Science and technology by their very nature require unconditional respect for fundamental moral criteria. They must be at the service of the human person, of his inalienable rights, of his true and integral good, in conformity with the plan and the will of God.

— *Catechism of the Catholic Church*, n. 2294

# *Catholicism and Ethics*

**Rev. Edward J. Hayes**
**Rev. Msgr. Paul J. Hayes**
**Dorothy Ellen Kelly, R.N.**
**and James J. Drummey**

**C.R. PUBLICATIONS INC.**
**345 PROSPECT STREET**
**NORWOOD, MA 02062**

**C.R. Publications Inc.**
**345 Prospect Street**
**Norwood, MA 02062**



NIHIL OBSTAT
Msgr. William E. Maguire
Censor Librorum

IMPRIMATUR
+ Most Reverend John M. Smith
Bishop of Trenton
September 19, 1997

The Nihil Obstat and Imprimatur are official declarations that a book or pamphlet is free of doctrinal or moral error. No implication is contained therein that those who have granted the Nihil Obstat or Imprimatur agree with the contents, opinions, or statements expressed.

Cover design by Jeff Giniewicz
Printed in the United States of America

ISBN 0-9649087-7-8

# Contents

## PART II
## MEDICAL-MORAL PRINCIPLES APPLIED



## PART III
## SPIRITUAL HELP FOR AND WITH THE SICK

# Preface

Month after month the media bring us word of startling experiments and findings in the fast-moving fields of science, biology, genetics, and bioethics. Whether it's the cloning of sheep, the fertilization of babies in the laboratory, surrogate motherhood, experimentation on human embryos, abortion-causing drugs, so-called partial-birth abortion, physician-assisted suicide, withdrawal of food and water from terminally ill patients, or tissue and organ transplants, the average person is overwhelmed by the possibilities of modern technology.

At the same time, however, the application of Catholic moral principles to these situations is lagging behind. Many people are forming their opinions on the basis of what they read in the newspapers or see on television, but these sources are hardly the most reliable guides on important moral matters.

Oftentimes individuals or families are faced with life-and-death decisions about loved ones, and they are not sure what to do. This book is not meant to be a complete textbook on medical-moral issues, but it can serve as a handbook to help resolve many problems with a medical dimension. It is written in non-technical language and would be a useful tool not only for individuals, but also for high school and college courses and for adult education discussion groups.

What is contained herein is based on the latest scientific and religious information at the time of writing. Scientific discoveries may raise new issues, but the moral and ethical principles we have enumerated will always be pertinent. These principles are taken from Sacred Scripture, the natural law, and the Magisterium of the Catholic Church.

We would strongly urge those seeking additional information to consult the many sources referenced in the book and in the bibliography. We call your attention in particular to the *Catechism of the Catholic Church*; the writings of Pope John Paul II, especially *Veritatis Splendor* ("The Splendor of Truth") and *Evangelium Vitae* ("The Gospel of Life"); and two Vatican documents: *Donum Vitae* ("Instruction on Respect for Human Life in Its Origins and on the Dignity of Procreation") from the Sacred Congregation for the Doctrine of the Faith and the *Charter for Health Care Workers* from the Pontifical Council for Pastoral Assistance.

We want to express our thanks to those who have read this book prior to publication and have shared their ideas and insights with us. We are especially grateful to Professor Gerald Williams, who has a Ph.B in Philosophy from the Angelicum in Rome and a Ph.D in Philosophy and Ethics from New York University. He is currently a professor of Ethics at Seton Hall University and professor of Medical Ethics at Kean College in New Jersey.

We are also grateful to Msgr. Harrold A. Murray, who has spent most of his priesthood in the Catholic health care field. He has served on the board of directors of several hospitals and acted as a consultant for national Catholic health care institutions because of his expertise in the field of medical ethics.

Something of the spirit and intent of this handbook is reflected in the words of Pope John Paul II to the First Plenary Assembly of Health Care Councils on February 9, 1990. Speaking about "the massive task of providing constant information about the directives of the Church Magisterium on the serious problems connected to medical ethics and scientific research," the Holy Father said:

> New frontiers opened by progress in science and technology, the so-called socialization of medicine and growing interdependence among people, situate the issues of health and health care at the center of a commitment to the advancement of human rights; and among these and fundamental to them, without a doubt, are those rights which regard the protection of life from conception to its natural end.

## BOOKS IN THIS SERIES

*Catholicism and Reason*
and
*Leader's / Catechist's Manual*

*Catholicism and Life*
and
*Leader's / Catechist's Manual*

*Catholicism and Society*
and
*Leader's / Catechist's Manual*

*Catholicism and Ethics*
(No Manual)

Additional books in this series may be ordered by writing to the address below or by calling or faxing (781) 762-8811. *Reason*, *Life*, and *Society* are $8.50 each and the manuals are $3.95 each. *Ethics*, which does not have a manual, is $9.95, and shipping and handling charges for all books are additional. There is a 20 percent discount for schools, parishes, and church groups, and 40 percent for bookstores. Major credit cards are accepted. Otherwise, send check or money order (U.S. funds only) to:

**C.R. Publications Inc.**
**345 Prospect Street**
**Norwood, MA 02062**

# PART I

# BASIC PRINCIPLES OF ETHICS AND MORALITY

Methodical research in all branches of knowledge, provided it is carried out in a truly scientific manner and does not override moral laws, can never conflict with the faith because the things of the world and the things of faith derive from the same God.

— Vatican Council II,
*The Church in the Modern World*, n. 36

Chapter 1

# The Nature of Ethics and Morality

In making moral choices, the morality of one's actions does not depend entirely on the sincerity of the intention or the evaluation of the motives, but it must be determined according to objective criteria drawn from the nature of the person and his acts. — Pope John Paul II to a Medical-Moral Workshop, January 20, 1990

The fundamental guiding principle which governs the conduct of all people has been given in the twofold rule laid down by Christ: love of God and love of neighbor. This norm should be uppermost in the mind of every person, but this general guiding principle must be spelled out in detail. How in my life am I to express my love of God? How am I to put love of neighbor into practice?

A simple answer might be to keep the commandments, but this is also a general answer. The specific obligations that we have are spelled out in the science known as "ethics." It is the purpose of this book to discuss thoroughly our moral obligations and ideals. Careful consideration will show them to be not burdensome duties, but rather a fruitful and joyful response to the norm laid down by Jesus to love God and neighbor.

## The Science of Ethics

**Ethics is the science which guides our judgment concerning the morality of human acts.** Medical ethics is the particular aspect of the science of ethics which guides our judgment concerning the morality of human acts in the medical field.

Ethics is a natural science. It employs the power of human reason. It is not based on the teaching of the Church, nor on the Bible. Being a branch of philosophy, ethics arrives at its conclusions by the use of human reason, philosophy's only tool.

Ethics is also a practical science. It is not studied just for the love of learning; all persons are bound in conscience to apply its principles to their conduct. Ethics is not a physical science. It does not deal with physical laws, such as water seeks its own level. It is rather a moral science, dealing with the free acts of people.

The material object of a science is the matter with which the science deals. In the case of ethics, the material object consists of human acts. Human acts are those actions performed by human beings, by men and women using their superior faculties of intellect and will, as opposed to those acts which we perform in common with animal and vegetative life.

The formal object of a science is the precise aspect under which that science deals with its subject matter. In the case of ethics, the formal object is the moral rectitude of human actions in relation to our natural end. In order to reach its conclusions, ethics draws upon the following sources:

- I. Human reason (primary source)
- II. Experience
  - A. personal experience
  - B. experience of others
    - 1. contemporary
    - 2. historical

Note that divine revelation (the Bible and the teachings of the Church) does not appear among the sources. Divine revelation is not a source of ethics, but is a check on its conclusions. If some conclusion of ethics is contrary to God's revelation, then the conclusion must be wrong since God cannot contradict himself.

## Ethics and Moral Theology

Ethics is also called moral philosophy. It is distinct from moral theology, although they bear a close relationship to each other. Ethics is based on human reason alone, which looks only to a natural end, while moral theology is based on faith as well as reason and recognizes a supernatural end.

The material object of moral theology is the human act — the same material object as ethics. The formal object of moral theology, however, is the morality of the human act in relation to our supernatural end. As God has decreed things, we cannot choose a natural end, but must strive for a supernatural end.

The sources which moral theology utilizes are these:

1. Divine revelation as interpreted by the Catholic Church
2. Human reason
3. Experience

The valid conclusions of the science of ethics regarding our conduct are accepted and confirmed by moral theology, which never contradicts the correct conclusions of human reason. The entire natural science of ethics is elevated and perfected by the supernatural science of moral theology. In practice, medical ethics is studied in conjunction with moral theology. In this way, the conclusions of human reason are verified and confirmed by the teachings of divine revelation.

In summary, ethics is the science which guides our judgment concerning the morality of human acts. "Morals" is human conduct in the light of ethics. Ethics is a science of ideals; morals is the application of ethics. It is therefore possible for a person to have good ethics and bad morals, as in the case of someone who knows the principles but fails to apply them in concrete cases. Accurate ethical principles and good moral conduct are both essential.

## The Basis of Ethics

The science of ethics is based upon the following truths:

1. Human reason is capable of discovering some truths.
2. God exists.
3. God is just.
4. A good life shall merit God's reward.
5. An evil life shall merit God's punishment.
6. We have a soul.
7. Our soul is immortal.
8. Our soul has the faculties of intellect and will.
9. The object of the intellect is truth.
10. The object of the will is goodness.
11. Our will is free and therefore capable of moral good or moral evil.
12. Good must be done; evil must be avoided.
13. An act is good when it conforms to right reason.
14. An act is evil when it does not conform to right reason.

These truths are proved in other branches of philosophy. In accepting them, the science of ethics does not show itself incapable of proving them, but merely leaves their proof to the departments of philosophy which are properly concerned with them. Each physical science accepts numerous facts established by other sciences. Engineering accepts mathematics; medicine accepts biology. In like manner, ethics accepts the fundamental truths which we have listed above.

## Ethics and the Catholic Church

Although ethics uses as its only tool the light of human reason, nevertheless one must find help in the moral teachings of Almighty God as revealed in the written Word of God and in Divine Tradition and as interpreted and explained by the living teaching office of the Catholic Church founded by Jesus Christ. Having arrived at the principles of ethics by human reason, we will often discover that our conclusions are already taught by divine revelation.

Thus, medical ethics in practice, as Catholics understand it, is not merely a philosophical science but a supernatural moral science and as such is subject to the authority of the Church.

Catholics believe that Jesus Christ, the Son of God, established the Catholic Church for the purpose of saving souls. They further believe that God's eternal law is the basis of every just law, and that it is by means of obedience to law that souls are saved. Therefore, the Catholic Church is intensely interested in every law, be it natural or positive, ecclesiastical or civil.

Indeed, the Church is more than merely interested. Having been appointed by Jesus Christ himself with the divine mission of winning souls to him, the Church is positively obliged to guide all people in the correct understanding of his law and to urge them to obey it. Moreover, since God has so charged and directed his Church, he will, because of his love and solicitude for souls, enlighten the Church in the proper and accurate interpretation of his law.

Jesus promised this help to his Apostles, and their successors, when he told them that he would be with them at all times, as long as the world would last (Matthew 28:20). It follows then that the Catholic Church possesses the authority to interpret all law insofar as it affects the salvation of souls. (For more on the founding of the Catholic Church, and the authority given to it by Christ, see *Catholicism and Reason*, a companion volume in this series.)

These principles apply no less to the laws of medical and scientific ethics than to any other laws. By obedience to the principles of medical ethics with the proper supernatural motive, it is possible to win a higher place in the kingdom of God. Conversely, by disobedience to them, it is possible for a person to lose his soul.

The Catholic Church, by reason of her interest in everyone's soul, is greatly concerned about the principles of medical ethics. The Church does not hesitate to interpret these principles with authority when she deems it necessary for the good of those over whom she has been given charge by Christ.

God is the Author not only of those laws which govern the operation of the physical universe, but also of the laws which govern the conduct of men and women. Since God cannot contradict himself, the findings of science must at all times be in agreement with the conclusions of sound philosophy and theology. There can be no conflict between moral and ethical principles on the one hand and the principles of physical science on the other. God is the Author of both, they complement each other, and both should go hand in hand.

This fact was recognized decades ago by Pope Pius XII, who told an audience of obstetricians and gynecologists on January 8, 1956:

> Although the Christian applauds new scientific discoveries and makes use of them, he rejects all materialism's exaggerated glorification of science and culture. He knows that science and culture occupy a place on the scale of objective values, but that, while they are not the lowest, neither are they the highest. In their regard, too, he repeats today as ever and always: "Make it your first care to find the kingdom of God, and his approval" (Matthew 6:33). The highest, the ultimate value for man is to be found not in science or its technical capabilities, but in the love of God and devotion to his service.

## The Norm of Morality

There exists an intrinsic and essential difference between moral good and moral evil. This seems like a simple and obvious statement of fact until we begin to analyze the motives and guiding principles being used by many people today. There are some who use the norm that current opinions and customs determine the

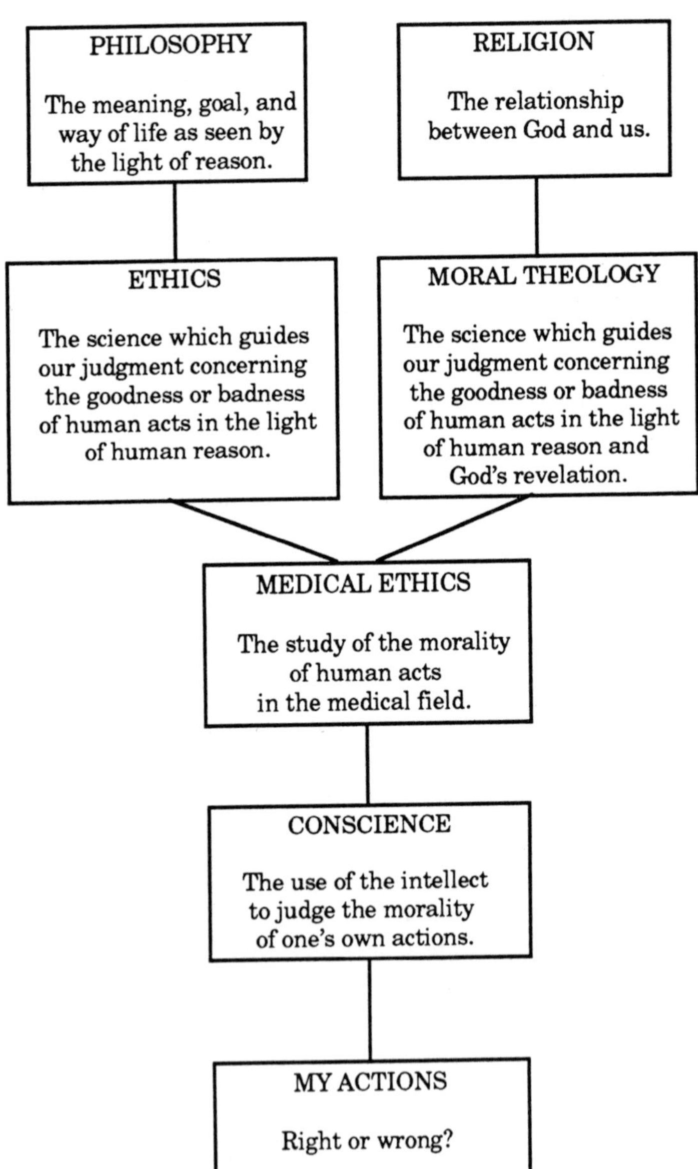


*Moral Judgment*

acceptable mode of acting or at least rationalize along those lines.

This is reflected in the not uncommonly heard phrase that "everybody is doing it." Those who use this excuse for immoral actions fail to acknowledge that right is right no matter how few believe it, and wrong is wrong no matter how many practice it. A morality that is based on majority opinion will lead to the eventual destruction of a nation.

It is also reflected in the notion that what is legal is moral. Thus, because the Supreme Court in 1973 legalized the killing of unborn babies by abortion for any reason during the entire nine months of pregnancy, some people believe that it is perfectly all right to do away with their offspring. They fail to understand that no court, no legislative body, no person can sanction what God has condemned.

Again, some people today consider as good and moral those things which in their opinion help society or others. This is a form of warped altruism that is used to justify such evils as abortion, euthanasia, and physician-assisted suicide because they relieve a person of some anxiety or suffering and relieve a family and society of some social or financial burden.

Still others regulate their actions according to what is useful for them at a given moment rather than what is objectively right or wrong. One of the best examples of this norm of expedience was a Roman governor two thousand years ago who passed a death sentence on an innocent Man. Pontius Pilate knew that Jesus was innocent ("I find no case against this man."), but because he was afraid the people might have him removed from office if he did not do their will, he ordered Christ to be crucified. It was the politically expedient thing to do.

How many politicians in our own time base their decisions and votes on expediency rather than morality? How many times have rulers of nations abandoned the ship of state to the winds of expediency, with results that are always confusing, frequently dangerous, and sometimes disastrous? This is the false theory of situation ethics; it denies absolute standards of morality and says that an action is right or wrong depending on the particular situation or circumstances surrounding the action.

Another category includes those who only do what they "feel" like doing rather than what they ought to be doing. Such is the person with bad teeth who will not go to the dentist. He has no doubts about what he ought to do, but a visit to the dentist might be unpleasant. Applying this standard to God's law is perilous, for a person who ignores the commandments or who attempts to justify principles and actions on the basis of what feels good will find himself far removed from God.

## The Theory of Consequentialism

There are also more sophisticated theories, such as consequentialism, which seek to justify objectively evil actions as morally good based on the intention of the person committing them and the consequences of the actions. However, Pope John Paul rejected such theories, saying that their proponents "are not faithful to the Church's teaching when they believe they can justify, as morally good, deliberate choices of behavior contrary to the commandments of the divine and natural law" (*Veritatis Splendor*, n. 76).

While intention and consequences can lessen the gravity of an act, the Holy Father said, they cannot make morally good something that is intrinsically evil. He quoted the *Catechism of the Catholic Church* (n. 1761) as stating that "there are certain specific kinds of behavior that are always wrong to choose because choosing them involves a disorder of the will, that is, a moral evil" (*Veritatis Splendor*, n. 78).

Referring to the Second Vatican Council's *Pastoral Constitution on the Church in the Modern World* (n. 27), John Paul cited as examples of acts that are always and everywhere evil, regardless of intentions and circumstances, homicide, genocide, abortion, euthanasia, voluntary suicide, physical and mental torture, arbitrary imprisonment, slavery, prostitution, subhuman living conditions, and degrading conditions of work (*Veritatis Splendor*, n. 80).

Thus, Christian morality is not a matter of current opinions, majority thinking, what is useful or expedient, or what our feelings tell us. Something is right if it is in conformity with human nature and right reason or is commanded by God; something is wrong if it runs contrary to human nature, right reason, or God's commands. Rape, murder, abortion, contraception, adultery, and euthanasia are wrong not because of statistics or public opinion polls or expediency or public apathy, but because they are intrinsically evil, i.e., they run counter to right reason and God's will.

Morality is intrinsic, objective, and unchanging. It is expressed in our life through a properly formed conscience. To attain such a conscience requires that we cultivate an analytical mind. We cannot allow our moral sense to be clouded by the false norms of morality so prevalent today. We must train ourselves to know the basic norms of right and wrong and tailor our actions accordingly.

## Discussion Questions and Projects:

1. What do we mean by the science of ethics?
2. Upon what sources does ethics draw?
3. How does ethics differ from morality?
4. Can a person have good ethics and bad morals?
5. What are some of the truths upon which ethics is based?
6. Why is the Church interested in medical ethics?
7. Why is God more important than science and technology?
8. How would you answer a friend who seeks to justify certain actions by saying:

   A. "Everybody's doing it."
   B. "If abortion is legal, then it's okay to have one."
   C. "Nobody should have to do something they don't feel like doing."
   D. "If euthanasia is going to mean less suffering and less cost for families and society, then it should be legal."

9. Since ethics presupposes a belief in God, a friend says, and some people do not believe in God, those people do not have to live according to a moral or ethical code. How would you respond?
10. How can you improve the moral thinking of your friends?

Chapter 2

# *The Morality of Human Acts*

"An evil action cannot be justified by reference to a good intention" (cf. St. Thomas Aquinas, *Dec. praec.* 6). The end does not justify the means. — *Catechism of the Catholic Church*, n. 1759

A human act is one that proceeds from the deliberate free will of a human being. It is an act that is deliberately and knowingly performed by one having the use of reason. Therefore, both intellect and will are in play. It is an act proper to us as humans. For example, if we decide that we need some exercise and go for a walk, we are performing a human act.

Quite different from a human act is an act of a man or woman. Such an act is not dependent upon intellect and free will. It is done by a human person, but is not proper to him as a person because it does not stem from those faculties which are peculiar to men and women, namely, intellect and will. In plain language, an act of man and woman is essentially an animal act.

Thus, if a person walks in her sleep, she performs not a human act, but merely an act of woman. All the acts of human infants are acts of man and woman because an infant does not have the use of reason; in other words, his intellect is not functioning. Breathing is an act of man or woman, as is spontaneously recoiling from the approach of a fast-moving and dangerous object, such as flying glass in an automobile accident.

In judging the morality of acts (whether they are good or evil), we will be concerned only with human acts, those involving the use of intellect and will, and not with the acts of man and woman, which have nothing to do with the moral law.

Every human act derives its morality from three elements: the act itself, the purpose of the act (sometimes called "the end"), and the circumstances surrounding the act.

## The Act Itself

It can be rather easily seen that, in order to judge the morality of a human act, we must first consider the act itself or the object of the act. This is "the primary and decisive element for moral judgment," said Pope John Paul in his encyclical on morality *Veritatis Splendor*, because it "establishes whether it is capable of being ordered to the good and to the ultimate end, which is God" (n. 79).

Visiting a sick person would seem, on the face of it, to be morally good. Certainly it is good as far as the act itself is concerned, but purpose or circumstances, such as using the visit to steal something, might make it evil. On the other hand, stabbing one's father with a knife is in itself a bad act, although it is possible to imagine circumstances when it would be morally allowable, such as in self-defense.

When the police arrive at the scene of a reported crime, they are sometimes forced to make a hasty judgment based upon the act itself. For example, if they saw you strolling leisurely near the scene of a robbery, they would have no apparent reason to arrest you, although they might want to question you about your knowledge of what happened. But if they saw you running from the scene, they would have good reason to think you had done something wrong and to pursue you.

On the other hand, if the police saw you break a store window, the act itself would be reason enough for an arrest. You might insist that you had broken the window for a good purpose, e.g., to call attention to a fire in the building, but you might have to explain that later in court.

In the moral order, as in the legal order, the first thing to be considered in passing judgment on the moral goodness or badness of any act is the act itself. We should note, too, that moral judgment must be based not only on the physical aspect of an act, but also and primarily on its moral aspect. If a person tells a lie, the moralist must base his judgment not on the physical act of uttering words, but rather on the telling of an untruth.

## Purpose of the Act

The second element in determining the morality of an act is the purpose, or end, of the act. The purpose of a human act is the reason for which the act is performed. In other words, it is the intention of the agent. A man lies about a doctor for the purpose of destroying the doctor's reputation. A doctor lies to a patient because he fears that the truth will disturb the patient's peace of mind. In each case, a lie was told, but obviously the guilt is radically different. What changed it? The purpose or intention of the agent.

It is important to remember that the purpose will not always change the morality of an act because, as noted in the previous chapter, some acts are intrinsically wrong (evil by their nature). Take, for instance, the act of murder, which is the unjust taking of a human life. A murderer may argue that he had a good purpose, such as the elimination of a drug dealer, but the murder is still wrong. Both the civil law and the moral law often follow this same line of thought on matters like this because the reasoning is based on the natural law.

## Circumstances Surrounding the Act

There is an old saying that "circumstances alter cases." That is true, and that is why the morality of a human act must be judged in the light of the circumstances surrounding the act. From the moral point of view, the circumstances of the act are those factors, distinct from the act itself and from the purpose, which may affect the morality of the act. Setting fire to a house at night is worse than during the day because the circumstance of darkness and the fact that the occupants are sleeping radically increase the guilt of the arsonist.

Murder, however evil, is so common these days that the average case causes very little public excitement. But if someone were to murder the President of the United States while he was delivering the State of the Union Address, there would be universal revulsion and condemnation of the murderer. The basic fact would be the same — a man was killed — but the circumstances are dramatically different.

So, too, in the case of a terrorist act like the Oklahoma City bombing in which scores of people died. The death toll was not much different from the overall murder statistics in the nation's major cities on a given weekend, but the circumstances caused a nationwide outburst of shock and the perpetrator was eventually found guilty and given the death penalty.

It is often impossible to give a direct and explicit answer to a moral question that specifies no circumstances. Priests are frequently asked in Confession, "Is kissing a sin?" But the answer depends on such things as who is being kissed, for what reason, and by whom. Another common question is whether a divorced person can receive Communion. No priest can give a fast yes or no to that question because it depends entirely on the circumstances, most especially on whether the person has remarried without having the first marriage declared null and void.

The questioner should not be surprised if the priest parries the question with another question. He is not trying to evade the question, but rather to obtain some circumstantial information, without which an accurate answer would be impossible.

## Principles for Judging Morality

In judging the morality of a specific action, some fundamental principles must be applied. What follows are some of the principles that should be kept particularly in mind. A more extensive discussion of these principles can be found in paragraphs 71-83 of *Veritatis Splendor* and in articles 1749-1761 of the *Catechism of the Catholic Church*.

1. An act is morally good if the act itself, the purpose of the act, and the circumstances of the act are substantially good. We say "substantially" good because an act may have minor shortcomings or defects and still be a truly good act. A person who declines to steal from an employer more out of fear of being caught than because stealing is wrong performs a good act, but not for the best of motives.

2. If an act is intrinsically evil, the act is not morally allowable regardless of purpose or circumstances. Murder, abortion, rape, adultery, racism are always evil. They are never allowed as a solution to a problem, no matter how serious the problem.

3. If an act is itself morally good or at least indifferent, its morality will be judged by the purpose or the circumstances. Walking is in itself indifferent. If a person is walking for exercise to improve her health, she is doing something good. If she is walking to a hotel to have sex with her boyfriend, she is doing something morally evil.

4. Circumstances may create, mitigate, or aggravate sin. They may change an indifferent act into one that is morally sinful. For example, striking a match is in itself an indifferent act, but striking a match in the presence of an explosive substance may be suicide or murder or both. Reading a wholesome book is a good thing, but becoming so engrossed in the book that one neglects to take care of a sick person is morally wrong.

Circumstances may also compound the sinfulness of an act. Fornication (sexual relations between two unmarried persons) is a grave sin against chastity; adultery (sexual relations with a married person who is not one's spouse) is a twofold grave sin — a violation of chastity and a violation of the marriage bond with the innocent spouse. To use obscene language is sinful; to do so in front of children adds the sin of scandal.

Circumstances may make a mortal (grave) sin out of a venial (slight) sin, or a venial sin out of a mortal sin. To steal five dollars is ordinarily a venial sin; to steal five dollars from a very poor person is a serious sin. Driving a getaway car from a bank robbery is ordinarily a mortal sin, but if the driver is being forced to do so under threat of bodily harm to him or his family, then his action is not sinful because he is not giving his free consent.

5. If all three moral elements (the act itself, the purpose, and the circumstances) are good, the act is good. If any one element is evil, the act is evil. If a reservoir is fed by three streams and one is polluted, the reservoir is polluted. If an automobile is supposedly in perfect condition except for a leak in the exhaust system, it is not in perfect condition. A person who never does anything wrong except to send hate mail to a neighbor is not a good person but a bad one.

## Conditions Affecting Morality

We are responsible before God only for truly human acts, i.e., those where knowledge and free will play a part. If these two faculties are not involved, we do not have a human act but only an act of man or woman. The objective goodness or badness of an act is one thing; the subjective accountability of the actor is another. It is easy enough to agree that the act of murder is bad, but just how guilty the murderer is before God is difficult to answer.

Since free will and knowledge always play a part in moral guilt, anything which might interfere with free will and/or knowledge must be considered in making a prudent judgment concerning the morality of an action, for certain factors can diminish the guilt of the person committing the act. There are seven particular conditions which may lessen or remove moral responsibility entirely: ignorance, fear, concupiscence, violence, habit, temperament, and nervous mental disorders. Let us examine them one by one.

**Ignorance** — In general, ignorance is lack of knowledge in a person capable of knowing. We are responsible in some cases

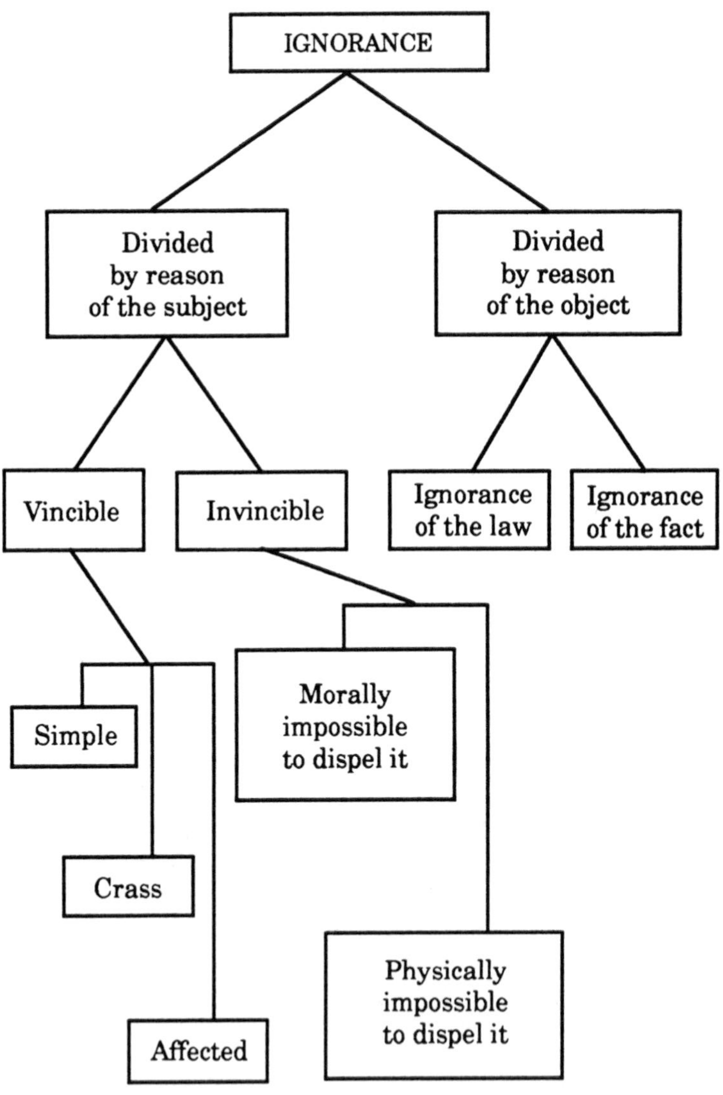


*Types of Ignorance*

for knowledge; in other cases, we are not. In other words, there are different types of ignorance and, before we can explain the moral principles regarding ignorance, we must distinguish the various types.

*Ignorance of the law* is lack of knowledge that a particular law exists, as when a driver does not know there is a 40-mile-per-hour speed limit for a particular road.

*Ignorance of the fact* is lack of realization that one is violating the law, as when a driver knows there is a 40-mile-per-hour speed limit, but does not realize that he is traveling at 55 miles per hour.

*Vincible ignorance* is that which can and should be dispelled. It implies culpable negligence, meaning that the person could know and ought to know. This can be divided into several categories:

*Simple vincible ignorance* is present when one makes some effort, but not a sufficient effort, to dispel the ignorance. A nurse who is unsure of what dosage of medicine to give to a patient refers to the doctor's order sheet, but is unable to read his writing. She knows the doctor is in his office, but does not bother to call him. In guessing at the dosage to give to the patient, the nurse is guilty of simple vincible ignorance.

*Crass vincible ignorance* is that which results from total lack of effort. A clerk in a convenience store does not know the price of an article brought to the checkout counter. The owner is in the back of the store, but the clerk does not want to bother the owner to find out the price of the product, so he makes up a price and charges the customer that amount.

*Affected vincible ignorance* is that which is deliberately fostered in order to avoid any obligation that knowledge might bring to light. For example, a person suspects that it is seriously wrong to miss Mass deliberately on Sunday, but he makes no effort to find out the truth.

*Invincible ignorance* is that which cannot be dispelled either because the individual is unable to secure adequate information, even after a reasonable effort, or because he simply does not know that there is any problem. In other words, he is ignorant of his ignorance. The person cannot be expected to take steps to enlighten himself because he is unaware that he is in need of enlightenment.

For example, an employee customarily tells lies by way of making excuses for minor faults and feels that, since they harm no one, they are in no way sinful. He is not aware that he needs enlightenment on this matter. Another individual may be confused in mind about a project, but after having made a reasonable effort to dispel his ignorance, and having failed to do so, he may proceed to act since once a reasonable effort has been made, the ignorance is invincible.

We may sum up the moral principles concerning ignorance by stating that invincible ignorance eliminates responsibility, while vincible ignorance lessens responsibility without actually eliminating it.

**Fear** — Fear is an agitation or disturbance of mind resulting from some present or imminent danger. It is one of the emotions. There are several types of fear.

*Light fear* is fear in which the evil threatening is either present-but-slight or grave-but-remote. An elderly lady experiences present-but-slight fear when she hears someone passing her door at night, but her fear is only slight because she knows it is probably her neighbor arriving home later than usual. A man who fears dying of cancer later in life is experiencing a grave-but-remote degree of light fear.

*Grave fear* is that which is present when the evil threatened is considered serious. It can be divided into two categories:

*Intrinsic grave fear* is that agitation of the mind which arises because of a disposition within one's own mind or body. The fear of cancer because one's parents died from cancer is intrinsic fear.

*Extrinsic grave fear* is that agitation of the mind which arises from something outside oneself. Under this heading come neces-

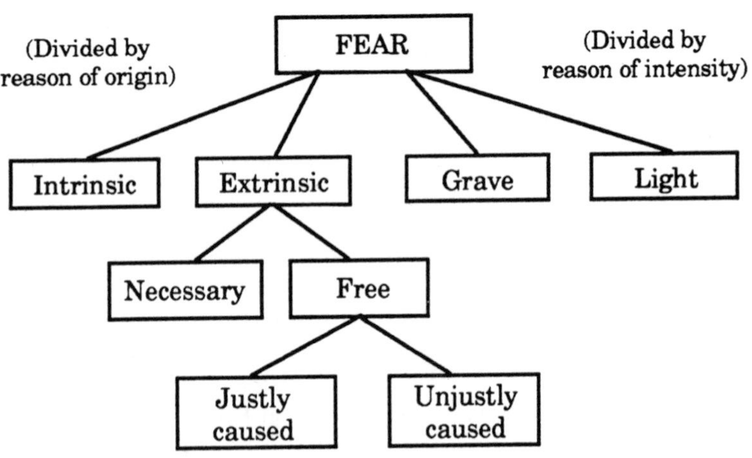


*Types of Fear*

sary extrinsic fear (that arising from some external physical law of nature, such as a tornado or a hurricane) and free extrinsic fear (that arising from the free will of another person, such as fear of a burglar in the house). Free extrinsic fear may be justly caused, such as a murderer's fear of being executed, or unjustly caused, such as an employee's fear of being dismissed if she does not keep quiet about a dishonest business deal.

Summing up the moral principles concerning fear, we may say that fear diminishes the voluntary nature of an act. However, one distinction must be kept in mind. Some acts are done because of fear and would not have been done if fear had not been present. Some acts, on the other hand, are done with fear present, but would have been done anyway. Any acts that are done, and would have been done anyway, whether fear was present or not, are clearly voluntary and, if they are morally wrong, the person is morally responsible.

Those acts which are done only because of fear are in reality freely willed and so carry with them some moral responsibility. However, a sinful act done because of fear is somewhat less free and therefore less sinful than an act done not under the influence of fear. Suppose a pharmacist gives some narcotics illegally to a person, fearing violence if she does not comply with the person's demand. Her act is free, but she is less morally responsible than if fear were not present.

**Concupiscence** — Concupiscence is the rebellion of the passions against reason. Or, to put it another way, it is a tendency of human nature towards evil. Concupiscence is the revolt of our sense faculties against the dominion of our higher faculty of reason. All of us perceive this revolt within ourselves. There are times when we feel strongly drawn to do something that we know would cause nothing but sorrow and regret to all concerned, even to ourselves, and yet we are strongly tempted to do it.

We seem at times like a man driving a team of unruly horses which pull in different directions and threaten to upset the wagon. Who is there who has not performed some regrettable act and then asked the question: "Why did I do it?" St. Paul commented on this inclination toward evil that we all have: "I cannot understand even my own actions. I do not do what I want to do but what I hate" (Romans 7:15).

The passions may be defined as the sense appetites of human nature reaching out toward their objects. Under this category would come love, hatred, joy, grief, desire, aversion, hope, despair, fear, courage, and anger. We often observe that a person who has had a prolonged stay in a hospital and suffered much pain may feel discouraged. This is one of the emotions of which we speak.

The passions are not evil in themselves. Parents may and often should exercise a just anger in order to discipline a troublesome child. Christ, who hurled forth the challenge, "Can any one of you convict me of sin?" (John 8:46), displayed a fearful anger when he rebuked his enemies and when he drove the moneychangers out of the temple. The sex passion, occasion of so much heartbreak, crime, and sorrow, is when properly used part of God's plan for giving citizens to a nation and saints to heaven. It is when the passions revolt against our nobler self that they become evil, and that revolt is called concupiscence (cf. *Catechism of the Catholic Church*, nn. 1762-1774).

Obviously, an evil action performed in the heat of passion is quite different from an evil action that is planned and calculated. Civil law recognizes this fact when it makes a distinction between murder in the first and second degree. Judges may not use the theological term concupiscence, but they often take it into account when they hear a case or pronounce a sentence. Such recognition of concupiscence is well-founded, for it does have an influence upon the morality of human acts.

Sometimes an individual deliberately arouses the passions, say by reading an obscene book or viewing a pornographic video before a date. In such a case, the moral guilt is increased rather than lessened. On the other hand, if the passion is spontaneous, culpability is lessened. A person who is leading a good life and is surprised by an unexpected temptation on a date may be less guilty in yielding to that temptation under the pressure of concupiscence than someone who deliberately fostered the temptation.

Concupiscence may be divided into two types: antecedent and consequent. *Antecedent concupiscence* is the sort which precedes an act of the will and is not willfully stimulated, such as sudden anger. *Consequent concupiscence* is that which is stimulated by the will, such as anger deliberately encouraged.

Since it is obvious that certain emotions, such as anger, grief, or discouragement, can so influence a person's state of mind that the use of reason and free will is affected, the moral principles concerning concupiscence need to be emphasized. Antecedent concupiscence lessens the voluntary nature of human acts and lessens the degree of moral responsibility accordingly. Consequent concupiscence, on the other hand, does not lessen moral responsibility; rather a person acting with consequent concupiscence is completely responsible for his actions. For example, a very depressed person who attempts suicide is less blameworthy because of his emotional state. But an employer who deliberately worked himself into a rage in order to intimidate a new employee would be fully responsible for his actions.

**Violence** — Violence is an external force applied by one person on another in order to compel him to perform some action against his will. In cases where the victim gives complete resistance, the violence is classified as perfect violence. However, if the victim offers insufficient resistance, the violence is classified as imperfect violence.

Perfect violence may be either physically or morally perfect. If a woman walking along a street at night is attacked, and she attempts to fight off her attacker with all the physical powers at her command, she has been the victim of physically perfect violence because she used every possible means to resist the attacker.

Now let us suppose that later that same night a man is walking down the same dangerous street and is set upon by a robber. At first he attempts to fight him off, but he soon realizes that further resistance will probably result in a severe beating, if not his death, and he will lose his money anyway. Deciding that discretion is truly the better part of valor, he ceases to resist and surrenders his money. Physically, he could resist further, but he is convinced that it would be useless. The violence of which he is the victim is known as morally perfect violence because he used all the powers of resistance that could be employed.

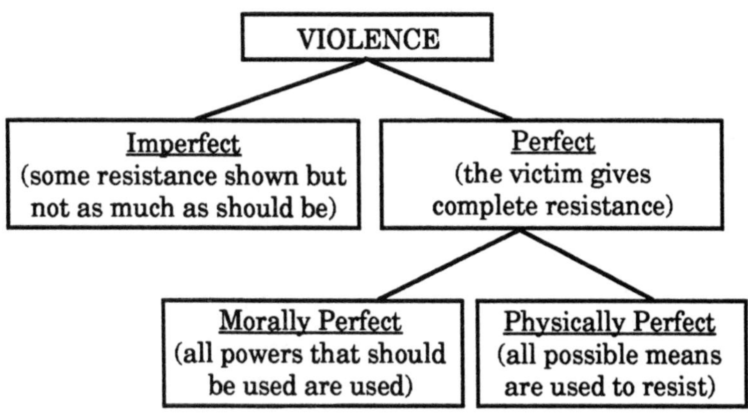


*Types of Violence*

A different situation regarding violence exists in the case of a woman working after hours in an almost empty building who is sexually harassed by her boss. The woman at first resists the man's rough advances and feels that stronger resistance might end the harassment. However, she then halts her resistance and gives in to him. The woman is the victim of imperfect violence because she showed some resistance to the attack, but not as much as she should have.

The moral principle concerning perfect violence is this: That which is done from perfect violence is entirely voluntary and there is no moral culpability attached. If an individual is a victim in the absolute sense of the word, no sensible person would condemn him. If the victim makes the judgment that resistance is utterly useless, she need not resist. There is no obligation to do what is useless.

Regarding imperfect violence, that which is done is less voluntary, and so the moral guilt is lessened but not taken away completely. Take the case of a captured soldier who has been subjected to some brainwashing but feels that he will be able to deal with much more. Yet, in order to be allowed to return to his cell and be left in peace, he decides to reveal military secrets to the enemy. This is a case of imperfect violence.

Perfect violence in this situation would occur if the soldier were severely beaten during interrogation and, while he was unconscious, certain secret papers were removed from his clothing.

**Habit** — The voluntary nature of human actions is also affected by habit, which is an inclination to perform some particular action. The habit is usually acquired by repetition and characterized by a decreased power of resistance and an increased facility of performance. A habit is sometimes called "second nature," meaning it is deeply ingrained in an individual as a result of constant repetition.

Some habits in our daily life, such as waking at a certain time, eating the same foods, sitting in the same spot in church every week, have nothing to do with morality. But others, such as cursing, lying, drinking, and telling obscene jokes, have very strong moral implications, as does habitual masturbation.

The Church has always taught that masturbation is "an intrinsically and gravely disordered action" because "the deliberate use of the sexual faculty, for whatever reason, outside of marriage is essentially contrary to its purpose. For it lacks that sexual relationship demanded by the moral order and in which 'the total meaning of mutual self-giving and human procreation in the context of true love' is achieved. All deliberate sexual activity must therefore be referred to the married state" (*Declaration on Certain Problems of Sexual Ethics*, n. 9).

However, that teaching is very much ignored or ridiculed these days by psychologists, sociologists, and those who use the media to dispense advice on sexual matters. They contend that masturbation is a normal part of growth toward sexual maturity and that its habitual nature takes away any moral culpability.

The document on sexual ethics, which was issued by the Sacred Congregation for the Doctrine of the Faith, concedes that psychological factors, including "adolescent immaturity, which sometimes outlasts adolescence, the lack of psychological balance, and ingrained habit can influence a person's behavior, diminishing his responsibility for his actions, with the result that he is not always guilty of a subjectively grave fault."

However, the *Declaration* said that this must be determined by one's confessor and added that the confessor should take into account "the habitual general conduct of the person concerned," the "care given to the observance of the special precept of charity," and whether the person was using the "necessary natural and supernatural helps" which "age-long Christian ascetical experience recommends for curbing passion and making progress in virtue."

In other words, habit does not destroy the voluntary nature of our acts. We are at least partially responsible for acts done from habit as long as the habit is consciously allowed to continue. If we take no steps to curb the habit, such as resorting to prayer, the sacraments, and practices of self-denial, then we bear some moral responsibility for our habitual actions. As long as we know the consequences of an act and do it repeatedly, we are consciously willing that which follows.

Suppose a person develops the habit of constantly misusing the Lord's name. He gets to the point where he doesn't even realize how often this happens, and may even be surprised when someone calls it to his attention. This habit got progressively worse over a period of time, and it will take time, and a conscious effort, to get out of this habit.

Just as we often take steps to break habits of eating or drinking or smoking to safeguard our physical health, so we should work just as hard to break habits that harm our spiritual health.

**Temperament** — Temperament is the sum total of those qualities which mark an individual. It is the total of native propensities or aptitudes which constitute a person's disposition. In fact, temperament can be loosely defined as disposition, and both heredity and environment play a part in its formation.

Some psychologists have attempted to categorize certain temperaments and their characteristics, such as pleasing and agreeable, domineering and strong-willed, pessimistic and brooding, and easy-going and lacking in initiative, but we don't pretend to know if these characterizations are accurate or if these are the only temperaments. We do know, however, that not every person can be fitted neatly into a particular psychological niche, and we know that a person's native disposition can affect the voluntary nature of his actions.

From the moral point of view, a person's temperament can somewhat lessen his responsibility for certain actions. For instance, a strong-willed person might be less guilty when he loses his temper than a normally easy-going person. A person who despairs easily might be more affected by temperament than someone who is optimistic. An individual who is cold and calculating will bear a different responsibility for his acts than the person who is pleasing and agreeable.

**Nervous Mental Disorders** — It is obvious that nervous mental disorders, such as hysteria, compulsive neurosis, melancholia, and hypochondria, can completely take away the voluntary nature of certain actions or at least lessen their voluntary nature because these disorders affect the operation of the intellect and the will. A brief discussion of certain mental states will indicate some of the moral implications involved.

*Neurasthenia* is a neurotic condition of debility characterized by feelings of fatigue, worry, and depression which may affect the activity of the will. In some cases, the subject finds himself unable to make a decision or unable to act on a decision already made. Loss of will power is technically known as *abulia*, which may be complete or incomplete according to the degree of will power lost. This is a true neurotic state, a pathological condition as opposed to bad will or lack of moral stamina.

*Hysteria* is a psychoneurosis characterized by emotional excitability and frequently accompanied by various symptoms, many of which have moral implications. These include angry outbursts, partial loss of memory, and a tendency to lie or steal or to indulge in immoral conduct.

*Compulsion neurosis* is a psychoneurosis characterized by compulsions and obsessions. Included in this category are such manias and phobias as pyromania (compulsive arson), kleptomania (compulsive stealing), claustrophobia (morbid dread of closed places), agoraphobia (morbid dread of open spaces), bacteriophobia (fear of germs), and pyrophobia (fear of fire).

These conditions may not only diminish or eliminate entirely the voluntary nature of acts, but also may excuse from the fulfillment of a positive precept, such as claustrophobia excusing a Catholic from attending Mass on Sunday.

Some might characterize masturbation as a compulsive behavior that would diminish the subjective guilt of a person. For more on this, see the material discussed under habit.

*Melancholia* is a mental disorder characterized by extreme depression and brooding. This pathological state should not be confused with a melancholic temperament, or with a temporary state of depression explainable in the light of a recent tragedy. Melancholia may give rise to inability to pray or to fulfill other religious duties, and to a difficulty in making decisions or carrying them out. At times the patient may develop feelings of guilt which have no basis in fact.

*Hypochondria* is a morbid anxiety concerning one's own health. It is characterized by imaginary ailments and, in extreme cases, can be marked by a tendency to suicide.

Sin and moral responsibility imply the use of intellect and will. Since nervous mental disorders can at times affect the use of these two faculties, moral responsibility for certain actions can be diminished or eliminated. In some cases, it is most difficult to determine moral responsibility, and we must leave such judgments in the hands of God. Caution should be exercised, however, lest there be an attempt to use a mental state as an unwarranted excuse for moral infractions.

There is an objective distinction between mental illness and moral turpitude. Not every terrorist or rapist is mentally sick; some are just plain evil. We must be careful not to overemphasize the role of mental disorders so as virtually to deny free will.

## Cautions Regarding Moral Judgment

Making a judgment about the objective morality of a human act in a concrete situation involves a consideration of all the conditions which affect morality: the nature of the act itself, the purpose of the agent, circumstances, ignorance, fear, concupiscence, violence, habit, temperament, and nervous mental disorders.

Every person has a conscience, but everyone also has the duty of enlightening his conscience to conform to the truth. At times this involves consultation with a person who has moral training. Even a highly trained and experienced moralist works with great care. It is certainly rash for a person untrained in moral science to make a quick judgment in an individual case, or to set himself up as an authority on moral matters. The wise person holds the opinions of orthodox moral experts in high regard.

Particular caution must be used in judging one's own personal situation. The old saying that no one should be a judge in his own case is a wise one. When faced with a personal moral problem, one should seek the advice of competent moralists who are loyal to the magisterial teaching of the Catholic Church.

## Occasions of Sin

An occasion of sin is an outside circumstance which offers a person an enticement or invitation to sin. The extrinsic circumstance may be a person (such as a bad companion), a place (a bar, theater, or beach), or a thing (an immoral book or video). In other words, any person, place, or thing which may lead to sin.

Occasions of sin vary in intensity and, for that reason, are referred to as either proximate or remote. Proximate or near occasions of sin are those which may easily lead a person into sin. Occasions which would tempt any normal person under normal circumstances are known as absolute proximate occasions. For example, an obscene book, magazine, or film is a temptation to all normal people.

Relative proximate occasions are those that would tempt only certain people. Thus, a tavern is an occasion of sin to a drunkard, but not to the average person.

A remote occasion of sin is one which is less likely to lead a person into sin, and this too can be divided into absolute and relative. An absolutely remote occasion, in which sin for the average person is possible but not probable, might include reading the daily newspaper. A relatively remote occasion, which could be sinful for some persons but not for others, might be a book on human reproduction. Contrast the reaction to such a book by a doctor compared to a curious teenager.

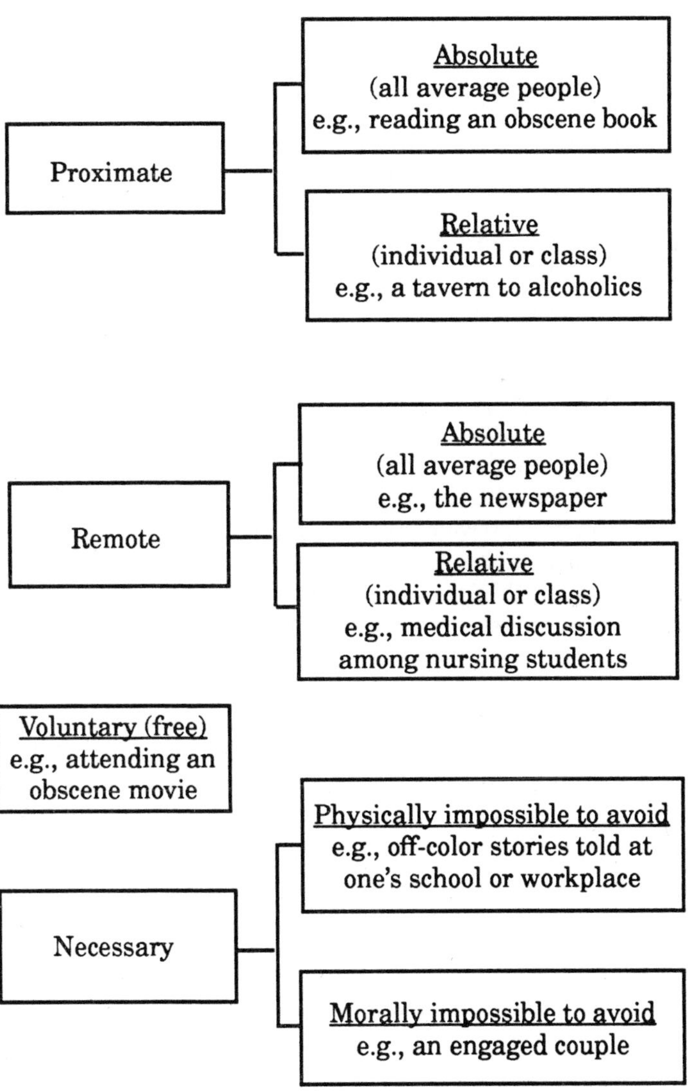


*Occasions of Sin*

There is still another division of occasions of sin, this one based on their necessity. Many occasions of sin are not at all necessary, such as going to a pornographic movie for recreation. Such an occasion is classified as free or voluntary. But there are some occasions that cannot be avoided. Law enforcement officials may have to view pornographic magazines or films in order to prosecute those who produce these materials.

Engaged couples sometimes find each other's company an occasion of sin, but they cannot completely avoid each other. A husband or wife may have a nagging or whining spouse who causes the other party to lose his or her temper, but they cannot live apart from each other. A doctor may find it impossible not to encounter some occasions of sin during the practice of medicine. What are these people to do?

We are morally obliged to avoid sin. Hence we are obliged to avoid all voluntary proximate occasions of sin, unless we have a sufficient reason. If a person finds himself in a necessary proximate occasion, he should take steps to render it remote. In the case of the person with the nagging spouse, the other spouse should exercise strong will power to keep his temper in check, avoid those things which prompt nagging or whining, pray for the other person, and do everything possible to minimize the occasion of sin.

When a person is in a necessary occasion of sin, God will give him special spiritual help to avoid the sin, provided that he seeks such help and sincerely strives to stay away from the occasion.

We have a light obligation to avoid remote occasions of sin unless we have a sufficient reason, but the reason need only be light. Since there is only a slight danger of sinning in such a case, and the temptation can easily be resisted, a person is morally allowed to read the newspaper or some popular magazine, even though some of the stories or advertisements may offer a slight temptation to sin. Actually, we could not expect to go through life avoiding all remote occasions of sin. Any attempt to do so would throw us into a state of scrupulosity, which is an unhealthy condition.

Let us pray that God will grant us the light to know what is right, the strength to do it, the wisdom to avoid occasions of sin, and the charity to give good example to others always.

## Discussion Questions and Projects:

1. What is the difference between a human act and an act of human beings?
2. What three elements determine whether an act is good or bad?
3. Why are some acts always wrong (intrinsically evil)? Give some examples of acts that are wrong by their nature.
4. How can circumstances change the morality of an act?
5. List the seven factors that can lessen or even remove moral responsibility. Give examples of two of these factors.
6. Explain the difference between invincible and vincible ignorance. Give examples of each.
7. Explain concupiscence and show how it can affect our moral choices.
8. Choose a bad habit of your own and suggest ways of correcting and overcoming it.
9. Explain what occasions of sin are and give examples.
10. If you were asked to debate the topic, "Moral principles should be changed to adapt to current-day situations," what arguments would you use to speak against this idea?

Chapter 3

# *Law and Conscience*

As the Second Vatican Council observed: "In the depths of his conscience man detects a law which he does not impose on himself, but which holds him to obedience. Always summoning him to love good and avoid evil, the voice of conscience can when necessary speak to his heart more specifically: 'do this, shun that.' For man has in his heart a law written by God. To obey it is the very dignity of man; according to it he will be judged (cf. Romans 2:14-16)." — Pope John Paul II, *Veritatis Splendor*, n. 54

The natural law is the code of moral conduct which reason indicates as conformable to human nature. For example, we are by nature adapted to live in society and, consequently, those actions are good which are conformable to the welfare of society, such as telling the truth, obeying lawful authority, paying one's debts. On the other hand, those actions are bad which will tend to disrupt society, such as lying, stealing, or rebelling against lawful authority.

We are by nature rational beings with a spiritual soul which should keep the desires of the body under proper control. Hence it is morally good by the natural law to be temperate and chaste, whereas it is opposed to the natural law to drink to excess or to seek sexual gratification outside of marriage. Further, as creatures of God, we owe to our Creator certain duties, such as adoration and worship.

## Properties of the Natural Law

The natural law exists in its subjects because it is an integral part of their very nature. Just as the laws of chemical reaction are inherent in the nature of the elements, so certain moral laws are inherent in human nature. A young child who has done wrong — lied, stolen, or disobeyed — feels uncomfortable, ashamed, or even frightened, even though he may never have heard of the moral law. His reason indicates that some things are wrong by their very nature. We say that such things are against the natural law.

When we speak of the natural law, we must emphasize that we are not talking about the laws of nature, which are physical and biological, but of the law of human nature, which is moral. In its *Instruction on Respect for Human Life in Its Origin and on the Dignity of Procreation*, the Sacred Congregation for the Doctrine of the Faith explained natural law this way:

> The natural moral law expresses and lays down the purposes, rights, and duties which are based upon the bodily and spiritual nature of the human person. Therefore, this law cannot be thought of as simply a set of norms on the biological level; rather it must be defined in the rational order whereby man is called by the Creator to direct and regulate his life and his actions and in particular to make use of his own body (*Donum Vitae*, n. 3).

If everyone, for example, could take the property of others at any time without fault or blame, no one would have any security in their property. All effort, all planning, would be useless. Initiative would be stifled, and the world would be in chaos. In other words, our natural reasoning powers tell us that stealing is wrong. Therefore, stealing is against the natural law. And the same can be said for abortion, adultery, murder, rape, lying, and a host of other evils.

Natural law is universal because, being based on human nature, it binds all human beings. It is immutable because human nature is the same at all times and in all places. Therefore, all acts contrary to the natural law, such as abortion, murder, theft, and artificial birth control, will always remain immoral. No human authority has the power to dispense from, change, or repeal any precept of the natural law.

## The Ten Commandments

The Ten Commandments are basically a summary of the principles of the natural law. The only exception is the Third Commandment, "Remember to keep holy the LORD'S day," which is a divine positive law. Men and women, even before God handed down the Ten Commandments to Moses, could tell right from wrong. But they drifted away from God, and he saw the need to put his law before them in a striking way, making it stronger and more explicit than the natural law they already knew in their hearts.

The entire natural law is not listed in the Ten Commandments. They list the major violations of natural law. For example, "Honor your mother and your father" embraces by implication all the obligations we owe to those in authority over us. The Commandments make no pretense at being an exhaustive list of every possible infringement of natural law. But they are a series of important guideposts, not mere suggestions, indicating the proper line of conduct in various phases of life.

Since we don't see the Ten Commandments enumerated very often these days, it might be well to list them here (cf. Section Two of the *Catechism of the Catholic Church*):

1. I am the LORD your God: you shall not have strange gods before me.
2. You shall not take the name of the LORD your God in vain.
3. Remember to keep holy the LORD'S day.
4. Honor your father and your mother.
5. You shall not kill.
6. You shall not commit adultery.
7. You shall not steal.
8. You shall not bear false witness against your neighbor.
9. You shall not covet your neighbor's wife.
10. You shall not covet your neighbor's goods.

The natural law is not meant to interfere with our liberty but to guide us in the proper use of our freedom. A railing is placed on the side of a narrow path along a precipice not to hinder people walking along but to protect them. They are free to step over or under the railing, but in doing so they only endanger themselves. The Ten Commandments are a set of God's directions on how we can avoid harm to ourselves and attain happiness both in this life and in the life to come.

## Positive Law

A positive law is a precept proposed by one in authority. In some instances, the authority may be God, as in many of the ceremonial laws of the Old Testament or the necessity of Baptism stated in the New Testament.

When God is the Author of a positive law, it is called "divine positive law." In other instances, the authority is human, as in the case of taxes in civil law or the obligation of fasting and Sunday Mass attendance in ecclesiastical law. This sort of law is called "human law" and can be changed by the same human authority.

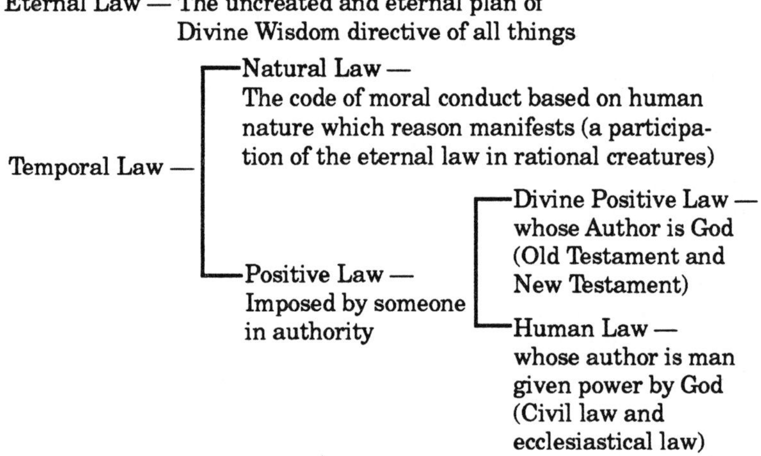


*Sources of Moral Guidance*

## The Judgment of Conscience

Conscience is a practical judgment of human reason concerning the moral goodness or evil of an action. In the words of the *Catechism of the Catholic Church* (n. 1778):

> Conscience is a judgment of reason whereby the human person recognizes the moral quality of a concrete act that he is going to perform, is in the process of performing, or has already completed. In all he says and does, man is obliged to follow faithfully what he knows to be just and right. It is by the judgment of his conscience that man perceives and recognizes the prescriptions of the divine law.

Conscience is not a separate faculty, a special little voice within us, whispering suggestions regarding our conduct. It is an act of the human intellect as to whether a certain action is right or wrong. Since it is an operation of the intellect, conscience is subject to the shortcomings of our intellect. Operation of the conscience implies knowledge, freedom, and reflection, all of which vary with each person and can result in different judgments by different individuals concerning the morality of the same act.

By keeping these things in mind, we can safely list and explain the various types of conscience. We will be concerned only with *antecedent conscience*, a judgment made previous to an act. We will not be discussing *consequent conscience*, which is a judgment made after an act.

## True and False Conscience

Considering the relationship of conscience to objective truth, conscience may be either true or false. **A true conscience is one which indicates correctly the goodness or badness of moral conduct. An erroneous conscience (sometimes called a false conscience) is one which incorrectly indicates that a good action is evil or an evil action is good.** Since conscience can be based on many things, from advice columns in the newspaper to the teachings of the Holy Father, it should be apparent that conscience is capable of error.

The human intellect is capable of being wrong, and just because the intellect is operating in the field of morality, or the fact that we give it a special name called "conscience," does not mean that our moral decisions are infallible. An error of conscience may occur because of some fault on the part of the individual. For example, suppose a person finds out that someone has made uncharitable remarks about him and feels that he is justified in making nasty comments in return. Such comments are not, in fact, justified, so the person is acting with an erroneous conscience.

If a person performs an act that is obviously a light sin, when his conscience tells him it is a serious sin, he has committed a serious sin. A boy who thinks it is a mortal sin to steal a small amount of money, and yet deliberately does so anyway, is guilty of a mortal sin. Conversely, if a girl commits what is objectively a serious sin, say, getting drunk at a party, but truly thinks it is only a light offense, she is guilty only of a venial sin.

It is important to recall, however, that no one can commit a sin when circumstances force him to act in a particular way. A Catholic who has been told by his doctor that he has pneumonia and must remain in bed on Sunday is not guilty of sin if he misses Mass, no matter what his confused conscience may tell him. No one is held to do the impossible.

## Certain and Doubtful Conscience

**A certain conscience is one which dictates a course of action in clear terms without fear of error.** It clearly labels as good or bad an action contemplated. A person tempted to seek revenge by committing a murder can clearly see that he is contemplating the performance of a gravely evil act.

**A doubtful conscience is one which leaves a person undecided as to the proper course of action.** A woman overhears members of a gang plotting a murder. She feels that she should report the matter to the police. However, she is certain that if she does so, the gang members will immediately realize that she is the informer and will try to kill her. Unable to determine what is the right course of action, she is the victim of a doubtful conscience.

## Lax, Scrupulous, and Tender Conscience

Conscience may err on the side of laxity, whereby a person can sometimes become persuaded that great sins are permissible. Such people often begin by rationalizing minor faults until their conscience becomes numb and incapable of proper direction. For example, a lawyer reveals a professional secret to some friends and considers the disclosure merely small talk. Or a couple routinely practices artificial contraception and excuses their conduct on the grounds that they already have two children.

Rarer than laxity of conscience is scrupulosity, whereby a person sees evil where there is none. For example, the seriously ill person who feels guilty for missing Mass on Sunday. Or the person who has had a past sin forgiven in Confession, but continues to think that the sin was not truly forgiven. St. Francis de Sales thought that scrupulosity had its source in pride in that some people are too proud to take the word of a priest, or even of the Lord himself, that certain actions are not seriously sinful. Such scrupulous thinking is wrong and a drag on the soul; it is to be avoided as much as lax thinking.

A conscience which forms a correct judgment with comparative ease, even in matters which involve fine distinctions, is known as a tender or delicate conscience. Many sincere people possess such a conscience, and others can also achieve this desirable goal with the guidance of a regular confessor or spiritual director. Those who listen attentively to the magisterial teaching of the Church will always know what course to follow on moral questions.

## Obligations Relative to Conscience

When our conscience is honestly and correctly formed, we are obliged to follow it. Here is the way Pope John Paul II put it:

> Like the natural law itself and all practical knowledge, the judgment of conscience also has an imperative character: man must act in accordance with it. If man acts against this judgment or, in the case where he lacks certainty about the rightness and goodness of a determined act, still performs that act, he stands condemned by his own conscience, *the proximate norm of personal morality*. The dignity of this rational forum and the authority of its voice and judgments derive from the *truth* about moral good and evil, which it is called to listen to and to express (*Veritatis Splendor*, n. 60).

Before following our conscience, however, we must make sure that it is correctly formed. The formation of conscience in a person who simply believes in God will be different from that of a person who believes that God sent his only Son, Jesus Christ, to suffer and die for our sins and to reveal to us how we are to live.

Furthermore, one who is a member of the Catholic Church is expected to follow its teaching authority since Jesus said: "Whatever you declare bound on earth shall be bound in heaven; whatever you declare loosed on earth shall be loosed in heaven" (Matthew 16:19). We believe that this power of binding and loosing was committed first to St. Peter and then to each of his successors down through the centuries because Jesus promised to be with his Church always, even to the end of time (Matthew 28:20).

"Christians have a great help for the formation of conscience *in the Church and her Magisterium*," said Pope John Paul in *Veritatis Splendor* (n. 64). "As the [Second Vatican] Council affirms: 'In forming their consciences the Christian faithful must give careful attention to the sacred and certain teaching of the Church. For the Catholic Church is by the will of Christ the teacher of truth. Her charge is to announce and teach authentically that truth which is Christ, and at the same time with her authority to declare and confirm the principles of the moral order which derive from human nature itself' " (*Declaration on Religious Freedom*, n. 14).

With this general norm in mind, we may give the following specific rules of conduct:

*An individual must always act in accordance with a certain conscience that has been sincerely and properly formed.* This is true even if the certain conscience is false. If one's conscience points out a particular action as definitely bad, even though objectively the act is good, the act must be avoided. Conversely, if the conscience points out an act as good and to be done, even though objectively the act is evil, that individual must perform the act.

*No one is allowed to act with a doubtful conscience.* The obligation in such circumstances is to resolve the doubt. If one is in doubt whether there is a law forbidding a particular action, one should obtain advice, first by determining the teaching of the Church and then by asking someone in a position to know the answer. A well-founded opinion obtained from a person other than ourselves is said to be based upon extrinsic reasons, or outside authority.

If I believe that medication A is the best treatment for disease B because an eminent specialist on disease B is of that opinion, then my well-founded decision to use medication A is based on good authority. If my opinion is based upon my personal analysis and judgment of the facts — presuming that I am competent and impartial — then my opinion is based on intrinsic reasons. So if I believe that a certain medication is the best because as a doctor I have made a thorough study of the matter, then the reasons for my decision are based on my own authority.

In any case, conscience is not a feeling or an opinion. It must be based upon truth, upon natural law, and upon positive law, both divine and ecclesiastical. Conscience is the umpire who "calls the play" when everything has been factored into a moral decision, and the decision of conscience is final. There is no appeal to a higher authority above a conscience that has been sincerely and properly formed.

But beware of self-delusion, especially in these days when all kinds of evil are being justified under the banner of following one's conscience. In his World Day of Peace message on December 8, 1990, Pope John Paul warned against such self-delusion:

> To claim that one has a right to act according to conscience, but without at the same time acknowledging the duty to conform one's conscience to the truth and to the law which God has written on our hearts, in the end means nothing more than imposing one's limited personal opinion.

Enlightenment of conscience at a later date has no retroactive effect. It does not change the morality of an act performed in the past when conscience was in error. As some people grow older, they begin to worry about their sins as children. They know now that some things they did were objectively very wrong, although to their young minds they did not seem serious at the time. To allow one's conscience to be thus concerned is a futile pursuit. God will not judge us in the light of knowledge acquired later. The subjective morality of our past acts has been determined forever. A newly enlightened conscience affects not the past but the future.

The sincere living of one's life in accordance with conscience puts a weighty responsibility upon an individual. But in going through life with all its difficult decisions, one is not alone. We have the Church which Jesus founded to guide us. We also have the following advice from the 1976 pastoral letter of the U.S. Catholic Bishops on the moral life (*To Live in Christ Jesus*):

> We must have a rightly informed conscience and follow it. But our judgments are human and can be mistaken; we may be blinded by the power of sin in our lives or misled by the strength of our desires. "Beloved, do not trust every spirit, but put the spirits to a test to see if they belong to God" (1 John 4:1).
>
> Clearly, then, we must do everything in our power to see to it that our judgments of conscience are informed and in accord with the moral order of which God is creator. Common sense requires that conscientious people be open and humble, ready to learn from the experience and insight of others, willing to acknowledge prejudices and even change their judgments in light of better instruction.

## Discussion Questions and Projects:

1. What do we mean by natural law? Can it change from one generation to another?
2. Commit the Ten Commandments to memory.
3. Which of the Ten Commandments is the most important and why?
4. Write a 300-word paper on one of the commandments, with examples of how it is violated today.
5. Explain the meaning of conscience and distinguish between a true conscience and a false conscience.
6. Describe how scrupulosity can be a drag on the soul.
7. Show how moral laxity can lead us into sin.
8. List and discuss the reliability of three sources of information that people consult when forming their conscience.
9. Why should we listen to the Church when forming our conscience?
10. How would you answer a person who tries to justify a sinful act by saying, "I was only following my conscience"?
11. Read sections 58-64 of Pope John Paul's encyclical *Veritatis Splendor* ("The Splendor of Truth") and summarize the Holy Father's main points.

Chapter 4

# The Twofold or Double Effect

Man is sometimes confronted by situations that make moral judgments less assured and decision difficult. But he must always seriously seek what is right and good and discern the will of God expressed in divine law. — *Catechism of the Catholic Church*, n. 1787

In our everyday life, we frequently perform actions which have more than one effect. For example, a family sends its children to a Catholic school. On the one hand, this results in a financial burden; on the other, there are the benefits of a religious education for the children.

Some actions have two good effects, such as going to church, which gives glory to God and good example to our neighbor. Some actions have two bad effects, such as drunkenness, which deprives the drinker of the use of reason and gives scandal to others.

Obviously, all acts that have only morally good effects may be done, and acts which have morally evil effects may not be done. However, what are we to do when an action has both a good effect and a bad effect? The answer can be found in what is known as the principle of the twofold or double effect. But before explaining this principle, some important distinctions should be pointed out.

## Some Important Distinctions

When we perform various actions, they are followed by various effects, some of which we desire (wish, intend, want, will) and others of which we do not desire but merely allow (permit, tolerate). A firefighter entering a burning building wills to extinguish the fire and tolerates inhaling quantities of smoke. An Olympic athlete puts in thousands of grueling hours training for an event in the hope of winning a gold medal. A person whose features are marred by a large nose undergoes a difficult operation, willing the correction of an abnormality and accepting the pain and discomfort of the recuperation period.

The same kind of analysis can be applied to moral conduct. Sin is an act of the will and, since this is so, we must distinguish between what is willed or intended and what is tolerated or merely permitted before judging the morality of an action.

Another distinction that must be kept in mind when considering the principle of the twofold or double effect is that there is a difference between performing a good act which has both good and evil effects, and performing an evil act in order that good may result. For example, if the officials of a state decree that a necessary new highway shall be built, they perform an act that benefits the common good, while at the same time working some hardship on those individuals who are required to move from their homes to make room for the highway. Both good and evil come from the same good act.

But if the government decrees that all retarded people shall be killed in order to decrease taxes, the good effect results from the evil act. The government performs the evil act of murder and taxes are lowered, but the desirable effect comes about only through the killing of thousands of innocent people.

Sterilizing a man or a woman so that they cannot add more children to their financially overburdened family is another example of achieving a good effect by engaging in an evil action; the benefit comes about only because of an immoral procedure. This is not permissible under Catholic moral teaching because an evil means can never be used to bring about a good end (cf. *Catechism of the Catholic Church*, nn. 1753, 1756, 1759, 1789).

## Four Necessary Conditions

Under the principle of the twofold or double effect, the science of ethics lays down certain conditions which must be fulfilled to justify performing an action that has both a good and bad effect. These are the conditions:

1. The action to be performed must be morally good in itself or at least morally indifferent or neutral.

2. The good effect must not come about as a result of the evil effect, but must come directly from the action itself.

3. The good must be willed, and the evil merely allowed or tolerated.

4. The good effect must be at least equivalent in importance to the evil effect. In other words, there must be a sufficient reason for permitting the evil effect to occur.

Although the conditions may sound complicated, all of us apply them frequently. A little boy cuts his hand, and his mother puts an antiseptic on the cut. This action has two effects: it causes the boy pain and it wards off infection. Although the mother did not realize it, she actually used the four principles above. She performed an action that was good in itself, namely, putting antiseptic on the boy's hand. The good effect did not come from the pain but rather from the use of the antiseptic.

The mother did not will to give her child pain, but only desired to help him. Finally, the good effect of preventing infection far outweighed the evil effect of the antiseptic's sting.

This is an easy application of the double-effect principle; it becomes more difficult when applied to more serious problems, especially those involving a great moral evil.

One classic example involves the right to life. A pregnant woman with cancer of the uterus is told by her doctor that an immediate hysterectomy is necessary to save her life. This procedure, of course, will result in the death of the baby she is carrying because the child is not developed enough to survive outside the womb. So the surgery will produce two effects: the good effect of saving the mother's life and the evil effect of ending the baby's life.

Is this operation morally permissible? Yes, under the principle of the twofold effect. First of all, the action of removing a cancerous organ is morally good. Second, the good effect of saving the mother's life is a direct result of the surgery, and not a result of the baby's death. Third, the intention of the doctor is to save the mother's life, not to kill the child. The death of the baby is an unintended side effect of the operation. Fourth, the saving of the mother's life is at least equivalent to the baby's death.

## When the Principle Does Not Apply

Now let us look at a situation which would not be permitted under this principle. A pregnant woman is suffering from pernicious vomiting, a condition that can easily be solved by aborting the child. However, such a solution is not morally permissible and violates the double-effect principle in the following ways:

1. The action is not morally good or even neutral; it is evil, it is an attack on innocent human life.

2. The good effect, namely, the health of the mother, follows from the evil effect. The mother is cured by the death of her child.

3. The evil effect is willed and not merely tolerated.

4. The death of the baby is not equivalent in importance to stopping the mother's vomiting.

It should be noted that such a condition can be treated with hospitalization, bed rest, the use of IV fluids, and antiemetic medications. There is no need for abortion, although this is still recommended in some circles. It is not morally permissible, however, because a good end never justifies an evil means. We may not do evil in order that good may come from it.

## More Applications of the Principle

*Case 1.* A commanding officer orders the bombing of a military base. He is aware that there are civilians on the base and civilian families living nearby, some of whom will probably be killed. Is the commanding officer acting morally? If we look at the four conditions of the twofold effect, we will see that he is.

1. Bombing a legitimate military target in wartime is not an evil act

2. The good effect of hastening the end of the war does not come about through the evil effect of killing civilians.

3. The commander wills only the destruction of a military target, not the death of the civilians.

4. Defending one's own nation, or another country, against an unjust aggressor in a just war constitutes a sufficiently serious reason to permit the evil effect of some civilian deaths.

*Case 2.* A married woman discovers that her pregnancy is not developing normally, that it is occurring in the fallopian tube instead of in the uterus. If the doctor does nothing, the tube will swell further and finally rupture, possibly causing the death of the mother. The only cure is to remove the tube promptly, which will save the mother's life and result in the death of the baby. Is it moral for the doctor to operate? The answer is yes.

1. The purpose of the operation is good, to remove a pathological organ which is a threat to the life of the mother.

2. The good effect of saving the mother's life does not come from the evil effect of killing the baby.

3. The surgeon does not will to kill the baby; his death is an unintended side effect of the operation that is merely permitted.

4. The good effect of saving the mother's life is at least equivalent to the evil effect of the baby's death.

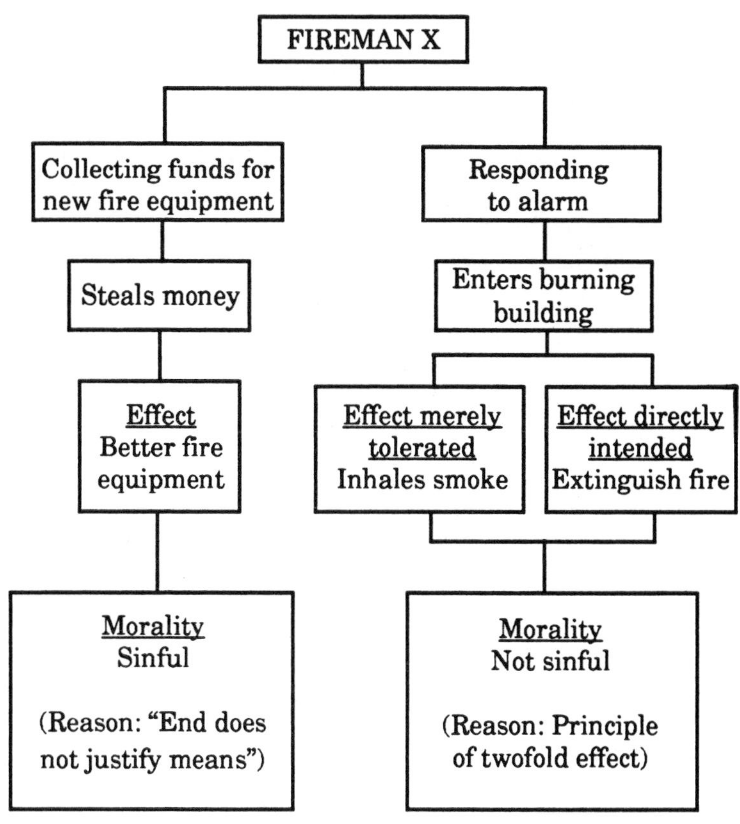


*The Twofold Effect*

*Case 3.* The leader of a nation engaged in war orders the execution of all inmates of mental institutions and nursing homes in order to devote the country's entire able-bodied population and resources to bringing the fighting to a quick end. Is this order morally justified? It is not, for the following reasons:

1. The killing of innocent civilians is not morally good in itself or even morally indifferent.
2. The good effect of ending the war would come from the evil effect of killing innocent civilians.
3. The evil effect is willed and not merely tolerated.
4. The good effect is not equivalent in importance to the evil effect, and there is not sufficient reason to permit the evil effect.

The principle of the double or twofold effect finds frequent and wide application today in the field of medicine. In most cases, the solution is obvious. However, in some cases there are very difficult issues to be resolved. When in doubt, one ought to consult a person who is especially trained in moral matters, and is loyal to the magisterial teaching of the Church.

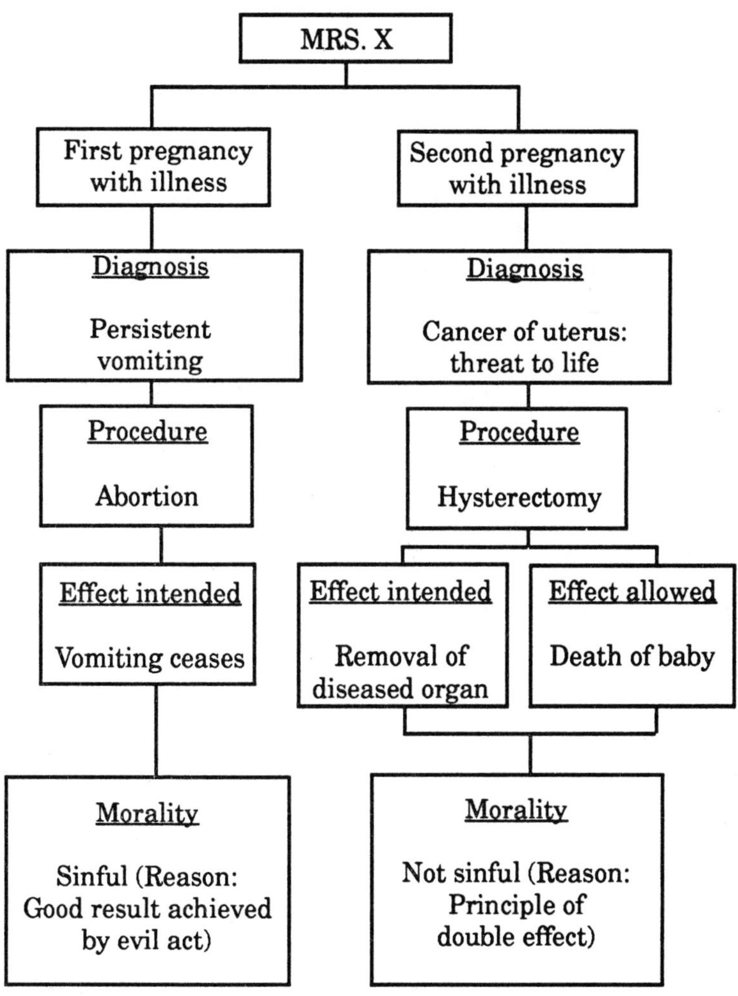


*The Double Effect*

## Discussion Questions and Projects:

1. Give three examples of actions that can have serious consequences.
2. How would you dispute the statement that the end justifies the means?
3. What are the four conditions necessary to invoke the principle of the twofold or double effect?
4. Which condition is the most important and why?
5. Make up your own example of the good and bad effects of a decision and show how it conforms to the double-effect principle.
6. Make up your own example of a decision with two effects and show how it fails to conform to the double-effect principle.

Chapter 5

# Moral Guides and Maxims

The natural law is nothing other than the light of understanding placed in us by God; through it we know what we must do and what we must avoid. God has given this light or law at the creation. — St. Thomas Aquinas as quoted in the *Catechism of the Catholic Church*, n. 1955

We are familiar with many sayings or axioms which help to express a truth or to provide some guidance in our lives. Phrases such as "A person is known by the company he keeps," or "Honesty is the best policy," or "Look before you leap" are generalizations in a popular vein which contain some wisdom or truth by which to guide our actions.

Similarly, there are many moral guides and maxims which, if rightly understood, can be a big help in interpreting the moral law correctly. They are based on the natural law, Church teaching, and common sense, and we shall discuss some of them and suggest ways in which they can be applied. The question of ordinary and extraordinary means, while discussed later in the book in connection with euthanasia, will be treated here because it has relevance in several of the following chapters.

## The Rule of Ordinary Means

Natural reason and the principles of Christian morality say that a person entrusted with the task of taking care of another human being has the right and the duty in case of serious illness to take the necessary means for the preservation of life and health. According to circumstances of persons, places, times, and cultures, one is normally held only to use ordinary means, that is, means that do not involve any unusually grave burden for oneself or for another person.

Some medical means are clearly ordinary, such as giving insulin to a severe diabetic, whereas others are extraordinary, such as undergoing a heart-lung transplant. However, there are various medical procedures which are not as clearcut and which require a thoughtful weighing of a number of factors and circumstances in order to determine in an individual case the distinction between ordinary and extraordinary means.

Most of those in the medical profession, as well as in the general population, wish to take every means possible and to make every effort to preserve life and health. This is commendable, but we need to emphasize that, normally speaking, there is no obligation to utilize extraordinary means. Let us consider some examples and apply to them norms which have been enunciated by the Church to guide the faithful in making medical/moral decisions.

## Ordinary vs. Extraordinary Means

Does a doctor have the right or is he bound, in all cases of deep unconsciousness, even in those that are considered to be completely hopeless in the opinion of competent medical personnel, to use modern artificial respiration apparatus? In ordinary cases, a doctor does have the right to act in such a manner, but he is not bound to do so.

The rights and duties of the doctor are correlative to those of the patient. The doctor, in fact, has no separate or independent right where the patient is concerned. In general, he can take action only if the patient explicitly, directly or indirectly, gives him permission. The procedure of resuscitation which concerns us here does not contain anything immoral in itself. Therefore, the patient, if he were capable of making the decision himself, could lawfully request it and, thus, give the doctor permission to use it.

On the other hand, since these forms of treatment can go beyond the ordinary means which one is bound to use, it cannot be held that there is an obligation to use them, nor that one is bound to give the doctor permission to use them. As far as the patient's family is concerned, their rights and duties generally depend upon the desires of the unconscious patient. Families are bound only to the use of ordinary means.

If it appears, therefore, that the attempt at resuscitation no longer corresponds to the real situation of the patient and constitutes in reality such an excessive burden for the family that one cannot in all conscience impose it upon them, they may lawfully insist that the doctor discontinue resuscitation attempts, and the doctor may lawfully comply.

This is not a case of disposing of a patient's life, or of euthanasia, which would be morally illicit. As Pope John Paul said: "To forgo extraordinary or disproportionate means is not the equivalent of suicide or euthanasia; it rather expresses acceptance of the human condition in the face of death" (*Evangelium Vitae*, n. 65).

Even when it causes an arrest of circulation for the patient, the interruption of attempts at resuscitation is never more than an indirect cause of the cessation of life, and one must in this case apply the principle of the twofold or double effect discussed in the previous chapter.

While we usually need not take extraordinary means to preserve life, there may be circumstances that make the use of extraordinary means mandatory from a moral point of view. For instance, a father or mother who is the only support of a family may for the sake of the children be obliged to undergo even extraordinary means to preserve life. The difficulty comes in determining just what constitutes ordinary or extraordinary means, especially with the advances in medicine.

One observer offers this explanation of the difference:

> Ordinary means what is well established and regarded as normal within the context in question; it is what we might expect a reasonable person to undertake and offers the possibility of real benefit to the patient. Extraordinary is anything which doesn't fit into this criterion (Kenneth Kearon, *Medical Ethics: An Introduction*, p. 36).

Another distinction has to do with how these terms are viewed by medical personnel on the one hand and moralists on the other. As Fr. Russell Smith has pointed out:

> In medicine, a means is ordinary which is (1) scientifically established, (2) statistically successful, and (3) reasonably available. If any of these conditions is lacking, the means is considered to be extraordinary. In moral theology, a means is ordinary if it is beneficial, useful, or not unreasonably burdensome (physically or psychologically) to the patient. There is a consideration of reasonable cost as well (*Ethics & Medics*, April 1995, p. 1).

Fr. Smith went on to say that "the common elements employed by theologians to determine whether something is ordinary means in a given case are: hope of benefit, 'common use' (that is, not experimental or exotic), 'according to one's status' (financially and psychologically), not difficult to use, and not otherwise unreasonable. The Church further teaches that while extraordinary means are not usually unethical to undergo, it is not morally obligatory that one undergo them (unless one is not reconciled with God or if the lives of others depend on the life of the patient) (*Ibid.*, page 2).

In addition to the writings of Pope John Paul and Fr. Smith on ordinary and extraordinary means, the *Catechism of the Catholic Church* presents this magisterial teaching:

> Discontinuing medical procedures that are burdensome, dangerous, extraordinary, or disproportionate to the expected outcome can be legitimate; it is the refusal of "overzealous" treatment. Here one does not will to cause death; one's inability to impede it is merely accepted. The decisions should be made by the patient if he is competent and able or, if not, by those legally entitled to act for the patient, whose reasonable will and legitimate interests must always be respected (n. 2278).

## Some Norms to Follow

In light of what has been said so far, and to put this subject in a practical and moral context, we set forth the following norms:

(1) In general, we must take ordinary means to preserve life and health; normally, we need not use extraordinary means. Moral theologian William E. May elaborates on this point:

> The decision not to administer life-sustaining (better death-postponing) technologies or to cease employing them is a choice to care for the dying person, to minister to his needs as a human being in the process of dying, and to make his dying an act at which human presence and human concern are of greater value than tubes. We can morally and, indeed, ought morally to allow human beings to die their own death, but there must be a sufficient or proportionate reason for making this choice.
>
> The principle of sufficient or proportionate reason (or good) is relevant to the care of the dying .... Associated with this prin-

ciple is the principle of intentionality, which means that in choosing to allow a person to die we do not set our will against his life by intending to kill him. When both criteria are met, when both of these valid moral principles are operative, we can rightfully choose to allow a person to die and to care for that person in his act of dying (*Human Existence, Medicine and Ethics*, p. 146).

(2) The medical procedure or equipment used have a bearing on a medical/moral decision. Thus, the use of a ventilator for a long period or experimental brain surgery would be extraordinary.

(3) The extent of the invasiveness of the human body must be considered. For example, the removal of an inflamed appendix compared to a heart/lung transplant.

(4) There is the risk to the patient. A person with a serious heart problem contemplating a three-hour operation under general anesthesia is confronted with a serious risk.

(5) The expectation of success is a factor in making the decision. A routine type of surgery with a high rate of success would be ordinary, while a new surgical procedure with a low success rate would be extraordinary.

(6) How burdensome will the procedure be to the patient and his immediate family? There might be an extreme financial burden, such as wiping out the family's resources or causing them to lose their home. There could be prolonged and serious emotional stress.

(7) Is the patient spiritually prepared for death? For it is here, as Pope John Paul said, that "the Christian truth about life becomes most sublime. The dignity of this life is linked not only to its beginning, to the fact that it comes from God, but also to its final end, to its destiny of fellowship with God in knowledge and love of him" (*Evangelium Vitae*, n. 38).

## Other Moral Guides and Maxims

**In Necessity Consider the Spirit of the Law** — One often hears it said today that the spirit of the law is more important than the letter of the law. This is usually said by people who are trying to justify a course of action that is contrary to the letter of the law. For example, the "spirit of Vatican II" is often invoked to support actions, whether in the liturgical, educational, moral, or ecumenical fields, that were specifically ruled out by the Vatican II documents themselves.

However, there are cases where it is reasonable to dispense from the letter of the law in the interests of necessity and safety. When Jesus was criticized for curing people on the Sabbath, an apparent violation of the laws imposed by the religious leaders of the time, he invoked the spirit of the law by reminding the Pharisees that if a person's sheep fell into a pit on the Sabbath, there would be no hesitation in pulling the animal out the same day.

"Well, think how much more precious a human being is than a sheep," Jesus continued. "Clearly, good deeds may be performed on the Sabbath" (Matthew 12:12).

A modern-day example would be a police officer who has orders not to go beyond the boundaries of his patrol area. But if he suspects that a crime is being committed a block away from his area, he may cross the boundary to arrest the perpetrator if there is no time to contact his superior for permission.

Regulations may forbid a nurse from putting a patient on her floor in restraints on her own authority. But if a disturbed patient becomes dangerous and threatens to hurt himself or others during the night, and no authorities can be contacted for a prolonged period of time, the nurse may exercise the spirit of the law and put the patient in restraints until proper authority can be reached.

**The Whole Is Greater than Any of Its Parts** — This is the principle of totality. It is usually applied in connection with whether one can lawfully sacrifice a part of the body, for instance, an arm or a leg, for the good of the whole body. The answer of course is yes since the body as a whole is more important than its individual parts.

**One Who Acts Through an Agent Is Himself Responsible** — A teenager asks a friend for a video that she knows is obscene. The friend, knowing that watching the video would be wrong, asks his younger brother to bring it over so that he will not be responsible. Actually, however, the friend is responsible for arranging an occasion of sin through another person. Another example would be a person who, knowing that contraception is immoral but wishing to give advice and encouragement to a friend in this matter, enlists another person to pass along the advice so that she will not be doing anything wrong. The first person is still responsible, nevertheless, because she acted through a third party as agent.

**No One Is Obliged to Betray Himself** — If a person commits a moral infraction, he is obliged to seek God's forgiveness and to repair whatever harm he has caused to the extent that could reasonably be expected. For instance, if a person stole a considerable amount of money, he should confess the sin and make restitution for what was taken. He is not obliged, however, to identify himself as the thief or to turn himself over to the police.

**The End Does Not Justify the Means** — One common fallacy in the moral thinking of many people today is that if we have a good purpose in mind, then whatever steps are taken to accomplish that purpose are justified. A family that thinks a patient's tranquility will be disturbed if he realizes that he is dying, and tells him a lie about his physical condition, is doing wrong. Their good purpose has been accomplished by an immoral means.

In any case in which an act is immoral, it does not become moral because it is done for a good purpose. To steal from a wealthy person in order to give money to a poor person is wrong. It is wrong for a doctor to administer a lethal dose of a drug to a patient in order to terminate his suffering and lessen the financial burden on his family. It is wrong to seek an abortion because a pregnancy would jeopardize one's professional advancement.

**Defects of Nature May Be Corrected** — If a child is born with six fingers on each hand, there is no moral objection to surgery that would remove the extra fingers. If a man has serious scars on his face from a fire, plastic surgery may be utilized. However, a woman may not undergo breast enhancement surgery with silicone implants if that could be harmful to her physical health and/or could be for a questionable purpose.

**No One Should Act as a Judge in His Own Case** — In making a personal decision about some course of conduct, our judgment is often skewed by nonessential details. We are usually biased in our own favor and cannot see things objectively. We may be either too easy on ourselves or, in the case of a scrupulous person, too hard. In such matters, it is prudent to seek advice from someone who will be more honest in assessing the situation.

**If One Is Willing to Cooperate in an Act, No Injustice Is Done to Him by the Act** — John knows some secret that may be embarrassing to reveal. Only James shares this secret, and he is obliged not to reveal it. However, the time comes when both John and James agree to tell George the secret. James is doing no injustice to John since John has cooperated in revealing the secret.

Or consider the case of a physician who wishes to test the effects of a new medication. He agrees not to charge for any services, treatments, or medications provided a patient volunteers to take part in the test. The patient willingly agrees, but the medication fails to cure his disease. He then criticizes the doctor for subjecting him to the new medication. But this is not a legitimate complaint and no injustice was done.

**A Very Little Is Equal to Nothing** — As noted earlier, the spirit of the law is sometimes more important than the letter of the law. Sometimes a minute violation of the letter of the law may be considered as no violation at all. For example, the employees in a particular hospital are forbidden to take medical supplies, but a worker takes two aspirin tablets for a headache. This is so small a matter that it is equal to nothing. Similarly, if a person finds a dollar bill on the sidewalk, he need not take steps to find the owner since the amount is so trifling.

**A Little More or Less Does Not Change the Substance of an Act** — A clerk in a pharmacy each week is in the habit of stealing bottles of 100 vitamins to give to friends. She then decides to take bottles of only 50 each week. This minor difference will not change the morality of her acts.

In the recovery room of a certain hospital, procedures require that blood pressures be checked every 15 minutes. Patient A is doing well and seems in good condition when Patient B is wheeled in in critical condition and needing special attention. The charge nurse, while attending to Patient B, omits one pressure check on Patient A. This need not trouble her conscience since Patient A is still being given excellent care. The omission is so small as to amount to nothing.

**Laws Imposing an Obligation May Be Given as Narrow an Interpretation as Possible** — Relative to the interpretation of laws, a law granting a privilege may be interpreted in as broad a way as possible, while a law restricting our liberty may be given the most narrow interpretation. The Catholic Church attaches automatic excommunication to the sin of abortion. But if a woman attempts an abortion and it does not result, she is not excommunicated, although she is still guilty of a serious sin.

**No One Is Held to the Impossible** — In the moral field, God does not expect us to do what is impossible or unreasonable. Take, for instance, the duty of returning stolen goods or money. A person who does not have the goods or money to return, but is sorry for his act and has received forgiveness in Confession, is not required to return the goods or money until such time as this becomes possible.

A nursing home employee who is told to care for an unreasonable number of residents, and who becomes worried that he is neglecting his duties because he is physically incapable of giving all the residents the care they need, should keep in mind that no one is held to accomplish the impossible.

**Passion Does Not Usually Arise from Things to Which We Are Accustomed** — Much of the regularly accepted clothing of our day would have been considered scandalous years ago and perhaps would have constituted a serious occasion of sin. Today's modest clothing (we stress the word "modest"), although more revealing than the attire of former times, does not constitute an occasion of sin because we are accustomed to it.

Basic morality never changes — adultery will always be a mortal sin — but what constitutes a temptation to sin may change according to circumstances. Something that would be a strong temptation to a teenager might be utterly boring to a gynecologist.

**Sacraments Are Meant for the Good of Souls** — The sacraments, as we know, are outward signs instituted by Christ to give us grace, or a share in the divine life of God. When we say that the sacraments are meant for the good of souls, we mean that, when in doubt, give the sacraments. For instance, in an emergency when there is doubt that a person is alive, the Anointing of the Sick should be conditionally administered. If there is doubt whether an infant is alive or whether it has been baptized, Baptism should be given at least conditionally.

**The Salvation of Souls Is the Highest Law** — In all things our ultimate question should always be, "Is what I am doing best for my own and others' eternal salvation?" The doctor who performs abortions may make money in doing so, but he must ask himself whether what he is doing is morally good and helpful for his eternal salvation. A nurse who is torn between assisting at immoral operations or losing her good position must ponder this question. And so must a family faced with a decision about a seriously ill or even terminally ill relative.

## Discussion Questions and Projects:

1. List three popular sayings/axioms (other than those in the chapter) that we often hear today.
2. Give examples of the differerence between ordinary and extraordinary means.
3. What persons should be involved in life and death decisions?
4. Explain how some medical procedures can be burdensome, dangerous, extraordinary, or disproportionate to the expected outcome.
5. Why is it important for a patient to be spiritually prepared for death?
6. Explain the difference between the letter of the law and the spirit of the law.
7. Why is it dangerous to act as a judge in your own case?
8. What does it mean to say that no one is held to the impossible?
9. Explain the significance of the statement, "The salvation of souls is the highest law."
10. Discuss the following situation:

> Some say that when judging medically extraordinary means, one factor ought to be the financial burden to the community (the hospital or nursing home, the HMO, the government). In light of today's atmosphere, which Pope John Paul has called a "culture of death," could this open the door to more widespread euthanasia, particularly since financial considerations are entering more and more into conscientious medical care? Should we be cautious in introducing this factor into medical judgments, especially since it is not mentioned by Pope John Paul in "The Gospel of Life" or in the *Catechism of the Catholic Church* (cf. the *Catechism*, n. 2278, and "The Gospel of Life," n. 65)?

Chapter 6

# The Morality of Cooperation

Anyone who uses the power at his disposal in such a way that it leads others to do wrong becomes guilty of scandal and responsible for the evil that he has directly or indirectly encouraged. — *Catechism of the Catholic Church*, n. 2287

The word "cooperation" comes from the Latin word *cum*, which means "with," and *operari*, which means "to work." Thus, cooperation means working with another in the performance of an action. The action may be good or evil, but moral problems arise only when the action is evil. So the principles spelled out in this chapter apply only to assistance in immoral actions, and the cooperation we are talking about may be divided into two categories: formal and material.

## Formal Cooperation

**Formal cooperation is that in which the cooperator wills the evil, either by an explicit act of the will or by actually sharing in the evil act itself.** Those who share in an evil act sometimes claim that they did so unwillingly ("I am personally opposed to abortion, but..."). If they were truly unwilling, and truly opposed to abortion, they would not have assisted in the evil act at all, say by voting for or promoting easier access to abortion.

Since we are never allowed to will evil, formal cooperation in evil is always sinful. The assistant surgeon who is actually performing some part of an immoral operation formally cooperates in evil. A person who contributes money directly to Planned Parenthood knowing that it is the largest abortion provider in the country is guilty of formal cooperation in evil.

## Material Cooperation

**Material cooperation is that in which the cooperator performs an act which in itself is not wrong, though it is used by the principal agent to help him commit sin.** This type of cooperation, as opposed to formal cooperation in evil, is not always wrong. Its morality depends on the proximity to the immoral act itself and whether there is a proportionate reason. Thus, material cooperation may be either proximate or remote.

Proximate means that which is closely connected with the immoral act. For example, if a bartender sells alcohol to a patron knowing that he will drink himself into oblivion, then the cooperation is sinful. Remote cooperation means that which is less intimately connected with the evil action. If the material cooperation is remote, e.g., the distributor who sells alcohol to the bar, the cooperation is morally allowable for a proportionately serious reason and is not sinful.

Here is an example of the various forms of cooperation that can result from the same scenario. A gangster who plans to murder a rival secures the cooperation of the local police captain, who arranges to have no patrol car in the vicinity while the crime is being committed. The captain's cooperation is formal because he wills the evil act.

The criminal tells one of his henchmen to prepare the getaway car by checking the gasoline and making sure that the motor is operating perfectly. This man cooperates materially but only remotely. Another member of the gang is assigned to drive the car. This man cooperates materially and proximately. A third man is assigned to lure the victim to an alley so the gang leader can kill him. This man cooperates formally by sharing in the evil act.

Now let us take these general principles of cooperation and see how they can be applied in the field of medical ethics.

## Formal Cooperation in Evil Never Allowed

While nurses usually follow doctor's orders, they have a right to refuse to carry out orders that they believe are potentially harmful to a patient. Thus, when the question of assistance at an immoral operation, say, an abortion, arises, it is entirely within the nurse's rights to act according to her conscience and refuse to assist in the procedure. If the nurse willingly takes part in the abortion, she is guilty of formal cooperation in evil.

## Proportionate Reason for Material Cooperation

Under what circumstances may a nurse materially cooperate by merely tolerating the evil? Since material cooperation consists in performing morally indifferent actions which make the operation possible, a nurse cannot directly assist at an abortion, i.e., hand the doctor the instruments that he will use to take the life of the unborn child. However, she may clean the operating room after the surgery, or care for the woman who had the abortion, if failure to do so would cost her her job and if she could not easily get another job.

The general rule, then, regarding material cooperation is that certain material cooperation in an immoral operation is morally permissible when a sufficient reason exists. While no medical condition presents a good reason for the performance of an immoral operation, certain circumstances may exist that would constitute a sufficient reason for some material cooperation.

For example, the fact that refusal would probably result in dismissal, combined with the knowledge that a new position would be very difficult to obtain in the near future, could constitute a sufficient reason for one's proximate material cooperation in a particular case, depending on the gravity of the act. On the other hand, the possibility of slightly hurt feelings on the part of fellow workers would not be a sufficient reason.

When material cooperation is frequent, a proportionately graver reason is required. An isolated instance of material cooperation in an immoral act is more easily justified than repeated acts. It is difficult to justify employment in a hospital that is notorious for constant performance of such immoral acts as abortion and sterilization, no matter how remote the cooperation. The same might be said for working for a company that produces drugs or devices that cause abortions. The more necessary one's material cooperation is to the performance of an act, the graver must be the reason to justify it morally.

## Nine Ways of Cooperating in Sin

Older moral manuals used to list nine ways that a person could be an accessory to sin. The late Fr. F.X. Lasance included the list in missals and prayer books as part of an examination of conscience before going to Confession. We don't hear much about these nine ways any more, but we list them because they can improve

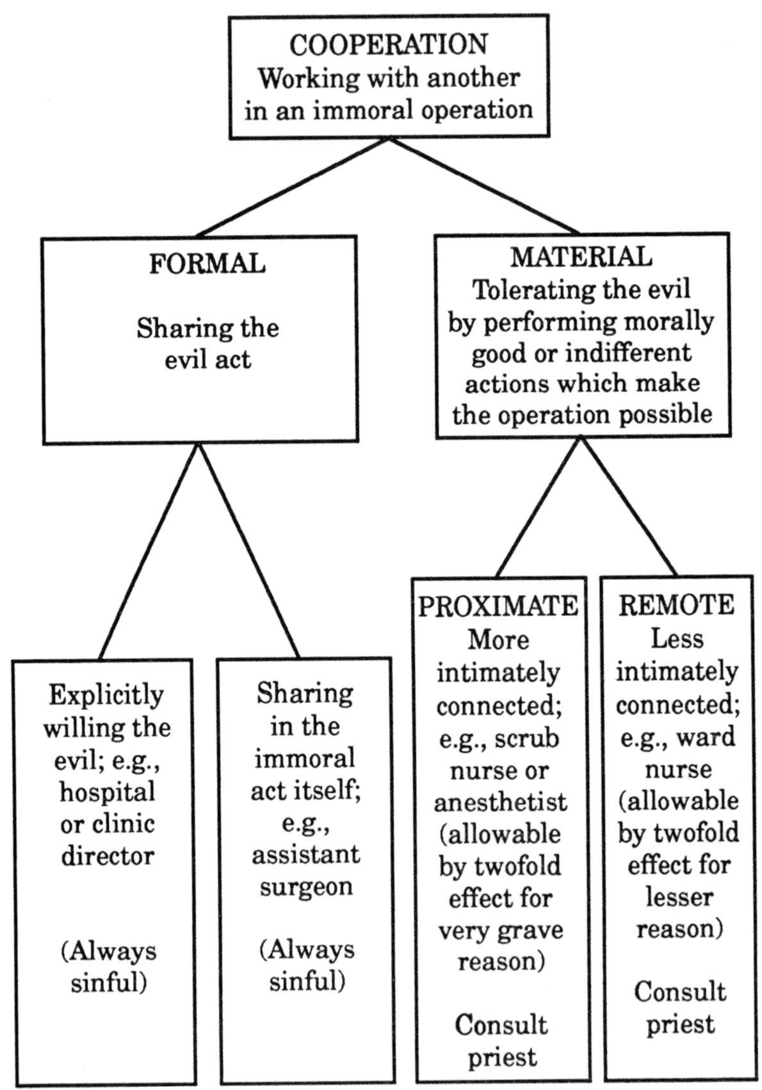


*The Morality of Cooperation*

our understanding of cooperation in sin. We have added some examples of each way:

1. By counsel (I would recommend you get an abortion).

2. By command (You must falsify that expense report or you will lose your job).

3. By consent (I think it would be a good idea for you to marry that divorced person).

4. By provocation (You should beat up that guy for stealing your girl friend).

5. By praise or flattery (You look sexy in that bikini).

6. By concealment (I'll tell your parents that you stayed at my house last night).

7. By partaking (The two of us can rob this company blind).

8. By silence (I won't tell anyone you stole that computer).

9. By defense of the ill done (You had no choice but to tell the doctor to inject your grandfather with a lethal drug).

## Resolving Doubts Regarding Cooperation

Between the obviously serious situations mentioned so far, and those which are clearly less serious, there are many situations that are not so easy to judge. It is not possible here to enter into a detailed discussion of all the possible cases that might arise regarding formal and material cooperation, so when there is doubt, one is obliged to consult a priest who is loyal to the Magisterium, or a trained and experienced ethicist, so that a definite norm of conduct may be arrived at to govern future situations.

One helpful and reliable resource in these matters is Professor Germain Grisez's three-volume work *The Way of the Lord Jesus* (Franciscan Press). The titles of the three volumes are *Christian Moral Principles*, *Living a Christian Life*, and *Difficult Moral Questions*. See especially Appendix 2 of *Difficult Moral Questions* (pp. 871-897), which is entitled "Formal and material cooperation in others' wrongdoing."

## Discussion Questions and Projects:

1. Explain formal cooperation in evil and give examples.
2. Explain material cooperation in evil and give examples.
3. Under what circumstances may a person cooperate materially in evil?
4. Which of the nine ways of being an accessory to sin is the most serious and why?
5. Choose one of the 200 problems treated in Germain Grisez's book *Difficult Moral Questions* and summarize his arguments.

# PART II

# MEDICAL/MORAL

# PRINCIPLES APPLIED

Science and technology are ordered to man, from whom they take their origin and development; hence they find in the person and in his moral values both evidence of their purpose and awareness of their limits.

— *Catechism of the Catholic Church*, n. 2293

Chapter 7

# *Principles Relating to the Origin of Life*

Man's life comes from God; it is his gift, his image and imprint, a sharing in his breath of life. God therefore is the sole Lord of this life: Man cannot do with it as he wills. — Pope John Paul II, *Evangelium Vitae*, n. 39

One of the least known facts about contraception is that, until 1930, all Christian churches were unanimously opposed to artificial means of birth control. And then, in August of that year, the Anglican Church in England, at its Bishops' Lambeth Conference, approved artificial contraception "in those cases where there is such a clearly felt moral obligation to limit or avoid parenthood, and where there is a morally sound reason for avoiding complete abstinence."

In December of that same year, Pope Pius XI sought to plug this break in the Christian moral tradition by reiterating the Catholic Church's ancient teaching on the immorality of contraceptive actions. Writing in the encyclical *Casti Connubii* ("On Christian Marriage"), the Holy Father, seeking to "preserve the chastity of the nuptial union from being defiled by this foul stain," proclaimed anew:

> Any use whatsoever of matrimony exercised in such a way that the act is deliberately frustrated in its natural power to generate life is an offense against the law of God and of nature, and those who indulge in such are branded with the guilt of a grave sin (n. 56).

A few months later, the Federal Council of Churches (USA), a predecesssor of today's National Council of Churches, endorsed "the careful and restrained use of contraceptives by married people," while conceding that "serious evils, such as extramarital sex relations, may be increased by general knowledge of contraceptives." This stance was sharply criticized by various Protestant churches, and even by secular sources, such as the *Washington Post*, which in an editorial dated March 22, 1931, said that the FCC's report "if carried into effect would sound the death knell of marriage as a holy institution by establishing degrading practices which would encourage indiscriminate immorality."

## The Years Since the Lambeth Conference

So what happened in the decades following the Lambeth and FCC declarations that led to the widespread use and promotion of contraceptives today, even by religious bodies? And why is the Catholic Church virtually the only Christian institution that not only refuses to change her teaching on this matter, but that continues to insist that her opposition to artificial contraception will never change?

A brief look at recent history, as well as a review of major Church statements from Popes and Councils, will provide the answers to the questions. Those looking for additional details should consult such important books as John Kippley's *Sex and the Marriage Covenant* (Couple to Couple League), Janet Smith's *Humanae Vitae: A Generation Later* (Catholic University of America), and Brian Clowes' *The Facts of Life* (Human Life International).

The next major breakthrough in the contraceptive revolution occurred in the 1960s. It was sparked by the advent of the birth control Pill, a Supreme Court decision that struck down laws that made the sale of contraceptives illegal, and the arrival of the sexual revolution that would have such devastating consequences in American society.

The Supreme Court's 1973 *Roe v. Wade* decision, which legalized abortion throughout the entire nine months of pregnancy and led to the extermination of a reported 1.5 million unborn babies each year since then, further immersed America in what Pope John Paul called a "culture of death" because it provided a backup solution to failed contraception. It was not a very big step for those who demonstrated their hostility to new life with the use of powerful contraceptive drugs and devices to choose abortion when these immoral tools did not achieve their stated purpose.

## Some Moral Guidelines

Before tracing the Catholic Church's unwavering opposition to artificial contraception, and before discussing the nature of contraception and the reasons why it is intrinsically evil, we need to recall some basic moral axioms that will help us to cope with the sex-crazed times in which we live. Sex is so overemphasized and distorted today, and our daily routine is so saturated with false images of what God intended when he gave us the beautiful gift of sex, that many people, even those who practice their religion faithfully, have acquired an incorrect attitude about sex.

Keeping the following guidelines in mind will help us to retain the proper Christian perspective in an increasingly anti-Christian culture:

1. Majority opinion is not the norm of morality.
2. Widespread custom or the conventional wisdom is not the norm of morality.
3. A good end does not justify an evil means.
4. If an act is evil by its nature, nothing can make it good.
5. We cannot allow our emotions to warp our moral judgment.
6. No one should try to judge his own case.
7. When the Church speaks, it is Christ speaking, the same Christ who said: "He who hears you, hears me" (Luke 10:16).

## An Unbroken Moral Tradition

The popular wisdom today is that contraception is a gift of modern medical and scientific research. But the fact is that contraceptive techniques are as old as human history. For centuries the term "Onanism" was used to describe a common form of contraceptive behavior. The act is named for Onan, one of the sons of Judah, who was struck dead by God in chapter 38 of the Book of Genesis for practicing *coitus interruptus* (withdrawal and ejaculation).

Modern defenders of contraception argue that Onan was killed not for spilling his seed on the ground but for failing to do his duty to his deceased brother, i.e., for his sin against justice. But, as John Kippley persuasively argues, three people in Genesis violated the Levirate (the duty of marrying a deceased brother's wife), but only Onan was struck dead by God. Why? Because only Onan engaged in the contraceptive act of withdrawal (cf. *Sex and the Marriage Covenant*, pp. 309-316).

Christian tradition has always taught that contraception is immoral. One of the earliest Christian writings, the *Didache*, which is a collection of the teachings of the twelve Apostles, said that "you shall not use potions" to prevent the conception of a child. St. Hipploytus of Rome, writing early in the third century, criticized in his *Refutation of All Heresies* those women who "take drugs to render themselves sterile."

St. Augustine, in his fifth century work *Marriage and Concupiscence*, condemned those who "procure poisons of sterility and, if these do not work, extinguish and destroy the fetus in some way in the womb." Husbands and wives who engage in such behavior, said Augustine, "are not married, and if they were like this from the beginning, they come together not joined in matrimony but in seduction."

In his work *Adulterous Marriages*, Augustine said: "Intercourse even with one's legitimate wife is unlawful and wicked where the conception of the offspring is prevented. Onan, the son of Judah, did this and the Lord killed him for it."

Opposition to contraception was reiterated by St. Thomas Aquinas in the 13th century and has been the constant teaching of the Church through the centuries, particularly in our own time, when the Magisterium has spoken forcefully against artificial birth control through Popes, an ecumenical council, Vatican Congregations, and the *Catechism of the Catholic Church*.

It should be noted, too, that Catholics have not been the only Christian opponents of birth control. Protestant leaders Martin Luther and John Calvin were both foes of contraception, and so have been many Protestant theologians since then (cf. Charles Provan's book *The Bible and Birth Control*).

## Pope Pius XI

As noted earlier, Pius XI reaffirmed in 1930 the Church's opposition to contraception in his landmark encyclical "On Christian Marriage." Responding to those who were "openly departing from the uninterrupted Christian tradition," the Holy Father said that "no reason, however grave, may be put forward by which anything intrinsically against nature may become conformable to nature and morally good. Since, therefore, the conjugal act is destined primarily by nature for the begetting of children, those who in exercising it deliberately frustrate its natural power and purpose sin against nature and commit a deed which is shameful and intrinsically vicious" (n. 54).

He said that "the Catholic Church, to whom God has entrusted the defense of the integrity and purity of morals, standing erect in the midst of the moral ruin which surrounds her, in order that she may preserve the chastity of the nuptial union from being defiled by this foul stain, raises her voice in token of her divine ambassadorship and through our mouth proclaims anew: any use whatsoever of matrimony exercised in such a way that the act is deliberately frustrated in its natural power to generate life is an offense against the law of God and of nature, and those who indulge in such are branded with the guilt of a grave sin" (n. 56).

## Pope Pius XII

Twenty-one years later, Pope Pius XII, in an address to Italian midwives on October 29, 1951, declared that "any attempt on the part of married people to deprive this act of its inherent force and to impede the procreation of new life, either in the performance of the act itself or in the course of the development of its natural consequences, is immoral; and no alleged 'indication' or need can convert an intrinsically immoral act into a moral and lawful one.

"This precept is as valid today as it was yesterday; and it will be the same tomorrow and always because it does not imply a precept of the human law but is the expression of a law which is natural and divine."

## Pope John XXIII

During his brief pontificate (1958-1963), Pope John XXIII wrote two widely publicized encyclicals — *Mater et Magistra* and *Pacem in Terris*. In the first of these documents, which was issued on May 15, 1961, the Holy Father called for respect for the laws of life. He strongly affirmed that "human life is transmitted and propagated through the instrumentality of the family, which rests on marriage, one and indissoluble, and, so far as Christians are concerned, elevated to the dignity of a sacrament.

"Because the life of man is passed on to other men deliberately and knowingly, it therefore follows that this should be done in accord with the most sacred, permanent, inviolate prescriptions of God. Everyone without exception is bound to recognize and observe these laws. Wherefore, in this matter, no one is permitted to use methods and procedures which may indeed be permissible to check the life of plants and animals" (n. 193).

Pope John XXIII went on to say that "indeed, all must regard the life of man as sacred, since from its inception, it requires the action of God the Creator. Those who depart from this plan of God not only offend his divine majesty and dishonor themselves and the human race, but they also weaken the inner fiber of the commonwealth" (n. 194).

While "the provident God has bestowed upon humanity sufficient goods wherewith to bear with dignity the burdens associated with procreation of children," the Holy Father said, "this task will be difficult or even impossible if men, straying from the right road and with a perverse outlook, use the means mentioned above in a manner contrary to human reason or to their social nature and, hence, contrary to the directives of God himself" (n. 199).

## Second Vatican Council

What saints and Popes had said before, the Second Vatican Council reiterated in its *Pastoral Constitution on the Church in the Modern World*, which was approved by the world's Catholic bishops in 1965. To get the full flavor of what the Council said about marriage and the family in the modern world, one should read sections 47-52 of this document in their entirety. We will emphasize those parts having to do with the purposes of marriage and the responsible transmission of life. Keep these passages in mind when someone tries to tell you that the "spirit of Vatican II" opened the doors to practices previously condemned by the Church.

In the section on the fruitfulness of marriage, the Council said that "marriage and conjugal love are by their nature ordained toward the begetting and educating of children. Children are really the supreme gift of marriage and contribute very substantially to the welfare of their parents. The God himself who said, 'It is not good for man to be alone' (Genesis 2:18) and 'who made man from the beginning male and female' (Matthew 19:4), wished to share with man a certain special participation in his own creative work. Thus, he blessed male and female, saying: 'Increase and multiply' (Genesis 1:28).

"Hence, while not making the other purposes of matrimony of less account, the true practice of conjugal love, and the whole meaning of the family life which results from it, have this aim: that the couple be ready with stout hearts to cooperate with the love of the Creator and the Savior, who through them will enlarge and enrich his own family day by day."

In deciding how to cooperate with God in the responsible transmission of human life, the Council said, married couples "will thoughtfully take into account both their own welfare and that of their children, those already born and those which may be foreseen. For this accounting they will reckon with both the material and the spiritual conditions of the times as well as of their state in life. Finally, they will consult the interests of the family group, of temporal society, and of the Church herself."

But in their manner of acting, the *Pastoral Constitution* said, "spouses should be aware that they cannot act arbitrarily. They must always be governed according to a conscience dutifully conformed to the divine law itself, and should be submissive to the Church's teaching office, which authentically interprets that law in the light of the gospel" (n. 50).

Continuing this train of thought in the following section of the *Constitution on the Church in the Modern World*, the Fathers of the Second Vatican Council said:

> Therefore, when there is a question of harmonizing conjugal love with the responsible transmission of life, the moral aspect of any procedure does not depend solely on sincere intentions or on an evaluation of motives. It must be determined by objective standards. These, based on the nature of the human person and his act, preserve the full sense of mutual self-giving and human procreation in the context of true love. Such a goal cannot be achieved unless the virtue of conjugal chastity is sincerely practiced.
>
> Relying on these principles, sons of the Church may not undertake methods of regulating procreation which are found blameworthy by the teaching authority of the Church in its unfolding of the divine law" (n. 51).

A footnote to this paragraph cites Pope Pius XI in *Casti Connubii* and Pope Pius XII in his 1951 address to Italian midwives as authentic sources of the Church's teaching on the responsible transmission of human life. Note, too, the emphasis above on a properly formed conscience, one that is submissive to the teaching authority of the Church, of which Jesus said, "He who hears you, hears me." And consider also the statement that the morality of human actions cannot be determined solely by sincere intentions, but must be based on the nature of the actions themselves, which, in the case of contraceptive acts, are contrary to the nature of the human person, as well as being contrary to the law of God.

## Pope Paul VI

While the Vatican Council was taking place, a special commission appointed by John XXIII and enlarged by Paul VI was studying the matter of birth control. Some Catholics were given the impression that a change was about to occur in the Church's longstanding opposition to artificial methods of contraception, and that in fact was the recommendation of the majority of those on the Birth Control Commission when they submitted their final report to the Holy Father in 1966.

However, on July 25, 1968, Pope Paul VI courageously reaffirmed the Church's constant and unbroken tradition over the centuries and earned for himself considerable opprobrium from those who had been lobbying for a change in the teaching. What the Holy Father said in his encyclical letter *Humanae Vitae* ("On Human Life") is so important and has such far-reaching implications that we will quote extensively from the document.

**On Responsible Parenthood** — "Conjugal love requires in husband and wife an awareness of their mission of 'responsible parenthood,' which today is rightly much insisted upon, and which also must be exactly understood .... In relation to physical, economic, psychological, and social conditions, responsible parenthood is exercised, either by the deliberate and generous decision to raise a numerous family or by the decision, made for serious motives and with due respect for the moral law, to avoid for the time being, or even for an indeterminate period, a new birth.

"Responsible parenthood also and above all implies a more profound relationship to the objective moral order established by God, of which a right conscience is the faithful interpreter. The responsible exercise of parenthood implies, therefore, that husband and wife recognize fully their own duties towards God, towards themselves, towards the family, and towards society, in a correct hierarchy of values.

"In the task of transmitting life, therefore, they are not free to proceed completely at will, as if they could determine in a wholly autonomous way the honest path to follow; but they must conform their activity to the creative intention of God, expressed in the very nature of marriage and of its acts, and manifested by the constant teaching of the Church" (n. 10).

**On Respect for the Nature and Purpose of the Marriage Act** — "These acts, by which husband and wife are united in chaste intimacy, and by means of which human life is transmitted, are, as the [Second Vatican] Council recalled, 'noble and worthy,' and they do not cease to be lawful if, for causes independent of the will of husband and wife, they are foreseen to be infecund, since they always remain ordained towards expressing and consolidating their union. In fact, as experience bears witness, not every conjugal act is followed by a new life.

"God has wisely disposed natural laws and rhythms of fecundity which, of themselves, cause a separation in the succession of births. Nonetheless, the Church, calling men back to the observance of the natural law, as interpreted by their constant doctrine, teaches that **each and every marriage act must remain open to the transmission of life**" (n. 11).

**On the Love-giving and Life-giving Meanings of the Conjugal Act** — "That teaching, often set forth by the Magisterium, is founded upon the inseparable connection, willed by God and unable to be broken by man on his own initiative, between the two meanings of the conjugal act: the unitive meaning and the procreative meaning. Indeed, by its intimate structure, the conjugal act, while most closely uniting husband and wife, capacitates them for the generation of new lives, according to laws inscribed in the very being of man and of woman. By safeguarding both these essential aspects, the unitive and the procreative, the conjugal act preserves in its fullness the sense of true mutual love and its ordination towards man's most high calling to parenthood. We believe that the men of our day are particularly capable of seizing the deeply reasonable and human character of this fundamental principle" (n. 12).

**On Faithfulness to God's Design** — "One who reflects well must also recognize that a reciprocal act of love, which jeopardizes the responsibility to transmit life which God the Creator, according to particular laws, inserted therein, is in contradiction with the design constitutive of marriage, and with the will of the Author of life. To use this divine gift destroying, even if only partially, its meaning and its purpose is to contradict the nature both of man and of woman and of their most intimate relationship, and therefore it is to contradict also the plan of God and his will.

"On the other hand, to make use of the gift of conjugal love while respecting the laws of the generative process means to acknowledge oneself not to be the arbiter of the sources of human life, but rather the minister of the design established by the Creator. In fact, just as man does not have unlimited dominion over his body in general, so also, with particular reason, he has no such dominion over his generative faculties as such, because of their intrinsic ordination towards raising up life, of which God is the principle. 'Human life is sacred,' Pope John XXIII recalled; 'from its very inception it reveals the creating hand of God' " (n. 13).

**On Illicit Ways of Regulating Birth** — "In conformity with these landmarks in the human and Christian vision of marriage, we must once again declare that the direct interruption of the generative process already begun and, above all, directly willed and procured abortion, even if for therapeutic reasons, are to be absolutely excluded as licit means of regulating birth.

"Equally to be excluded, as the teaching authority of the Church has frequently declared, is direct sterilization, whether perpetual or temporary, whether of the man or of the woman. **Similarly excluded is every action which, either in anticipation of the conjugal act, or in its accomplishment, or in the development of its natural consequences, proposes, whether as an end or as a means, to render procreation impossible.**

"To justify conjugal acts made intentionally infecund, one cannot invoke as valid reasons the lesser evil, or the fact that such acts would constitute a whole together with the fecund acts already performed or to follow later, and hence would share in one and the same moral goodness.

"In truth, if it is sometimes licit to tolerate a lesser evil in order to avoid a greater evil or to promote a greater good, it is not licit, even for the gravest reasons, to do evil so that good may follow therefrom, that is, to make into the object of a positive act of the will something which is intrinsically disordered and hence unworthy of the human person, even when the intention is to safeguard or promote individual, family, or social well-being" (n. 14).

**On the Licitness of Therapeutic Means (Principle of Twofold or Double Effect)**— "The Church, on the contrary, does not at all consider illicit the use of those therapeutic means truly necessary to cure diseases of the organism, even if an impediment to procreation, which may be foreseen, should result therefrom, provided such impediment is not, for whatever motive, directly willed" (n. 15).

**Licitness of Natural Family Planning** — "If, then, there are serious motives to space out births, which derive from the physical or psychological conditions of husband and wife, or from external conditions, the Church teaches that it is then licit to take into account the natural rhythms immanent in the generative functions for the use of marriage in the infecund periods only, and in this way to regulate birth without offending the moral principles which have been recalled earlier.

"The Church is coherent with herself when she considers recourse to the infecund periods to be licit, while at the same time condemning, as being always illicit, the use of means directly contrary to fecundation, even if such use is inspired by reasons which may appear honest and serious. In reality, there are essential differences between the two cases: in the former, the married couples make legitimate use of a natural disposition; in the latter, they impede the development of natural processes" (n. 16).

**Prediction of Grave Consequences** — "Upright men can even better convince themselves of the solid grounds on which the teaching of the Church in this field is based if they care to reflect upon the consequences of methods of artificial birth control. Let them consider, first of all, how wide and easy a road would thus be opened up towards conjugal infidelity and the general lowering of morality. Not much experience is needed in order to know human weakness, and to understand that men — especially the young, who are so vulnerable on this point — have need of encouragement to be faithful to the moral law, so that they must not be offered some easy means of eluding its observance.

"It is also to be feared that the man, growing used to the employment of anti-contraceptive practices, may finally lose respect for the woman and, no longer caring for her physical and psychological equilibrium, may come to the point of considering her as a mere instrument of selfish enjoyment, and no longer as his respected and beloved companion.

"Let it be considered also that a dangerous weapon would thus be placed in the hands of those public authorities who take no heed of moral exigencies. Who could blame a government for applying to the solution of the problems of the community those means acknowledged to be licit for married couples in the solution of a family problem? Who will stop rulers from favoring, from even imposing upon their peoples, if they were to consider it necessary, the method of contraception which they judge to be most efficacious?

"In such a way men, wishing to avoid individual, family, or social difficulties encountered in the observance of the divine law, would reach the point of placing at the mercy of the intervention of public authority the most personal and most reserved sector of conjugal intimacy" (n. 17).

**These Teachings Are not Church Laws** — "It can be foreseen that this teaching will not be easily received by all. Too numerous are those voices — amplified by the modern means of propaganda — which are contrary to the voice of the Church. To tell the truth, the Church is not surprised to be made, like her divine Founder, a 'sign of contradiction,' yet she does not because of this cease to proclaim with humble firmness the entire moral law, both natural and evangelical. **Of such laws the Church was not the author, nor consequently can she be their arbiter; she is only their depository and their intepreter,** without ever being able to declare to be licit that which is not so by reason of its intimate and unchangeable opposition to the true good of man.

"In defending conjugal morals in their integral wholeness, the Church knows that she contributes towards the establishment of a truly human civilization; she engages man not to abdicate from his own responsibility in order to rely on technical means; by that very fact she defends the dignity of man and wife. Faithful to both the teaching and the example of the Savior, she shows herself to be the sincere and disinterested friend of men, whom she wishes to help, even during their earthly sojourn, 'to share as sons in the life of the living God, the Father of all men' " (n. 18).

**To Those in the Field of Science** — "We wish now to express our encouragement to men of science, who 'can considerably advance the welfare of marriage and family, along with peace of conscience, if by pooling their efforts they labor to explain more thoroughly the various conditions favoring a proper regulation of births.'

"It is particularly desirable that, according to the wish already expressed by Pope Pius XII, medical science succeed in providing a sufficiently secure basis for a regulation of birth, founded on the observance of natural rhythms. In this way, scientists and especially Catholic scientists will contribute to demonstrate in actual fact that, as the Church teaches, 'a true contradiction cannot exist between the divine laws pertaining to the transmission of life and those pertaining to the fostering of authentic conjugal love' " (n. 24).

**To Christian Husband and Wives** — "We do not at all intend to hide the sometimes serious difficulties inherent in the life of Christian married persons; for them as for everyone else, 'the gate is narrow and the way is hard that leads to life.' But the hope of that life must illuminate their way, as with courage they strive to live with wisdom, justice, and piety in this present time, knowing that the figure of this world passes away.

"Let married couples, then, face up to the efforts needed, supported by the faith and the hope which 'do not disappoint ... because God's love has been poured into our hearts through the Holy Spirit, who has been given to us.' Let them implore divine assistance by persevering prayer; above all, let them draw from the source of grace and charity in the Eucharist. And if sin should still keep its hold over them, let them not be discouraged, but rather have recourse with humble perseverance to the mercy of God, which is poured forth in the sacrament of Penance.

"In this way they will be enabled to achieve the fullness of conjugal life described by the Apostle: 'Husbands, love your wives, as Christ loved the Church .... Husbands should love their wives as their own bodies. He who loves his wife loves himself. For no man ever hates his own flesh, but nourishes and cherishes it, as Christ does the Church .... This is a great mystery, and I mean in reference to Christ and the Church. However, let each one of you love his wife as himself, and let the wife see that she respects her husband' [Ephesians 5:25, 28-29, 32-33]" (n. 25).

**To Doctors and Medical Personnel** — "We hold those physicians and medical personnel in the highest esteem who, in the exercise of their profession, value above every human interest the superior demands of their Christian vocation. Let them persevere, therefore, in promoting on every occasion the discovery of solutions inspired by faith and right reason; let them strive to arouse this conviction and this respect in their associates. Let them also consider as their proper professional duty the task of acquiring all the knowledge needed in this delicate sector so as to be able to give to those married persons who consult them wise counsel and healthy direction, such as they have a right to expect" (n. 27).

**To Priests** — "Beloved priest sons, by vocation you are the counselors and spiritual guides of individual persons and of families. We now turn to you with confidence. Your first task, especially in the case of those who teach moral theology, is to expound the Church's teaching on marriage without ambiguity. Be the first to give, in the exercise of your ministry, the example of loyal internal and external obedience to the teaching authority of the Church. That obedience, as you know well, obliges not only because of the reasons adduced, but rather because of the light of the Holy Spirit, which is given in a particular way to the pastors of the Church in order that they may illustrate the truth.

"You know, too, that it is of the utmost importance, for peace of consciences and for the unity of the Christian people, that in the field of morals as well as that of dogma, all should attend to the Magisterium of the Church, and all should speak the same language. Hence, with all our heart we renew to you the heartfelt plea of the great Apostle Paul: 'I appeal to you, brethren, by the name of our Lord Jesus Christ, that all of you agree and that there be no dissensions among you, but that you be united in the same mind and the same judgment' (n. 28).

"To diminish in no way the saving teaching of Christ constitutes an eminent form of charity for souls. But this must ever be accompanied by patience and goodness, such as the Lord Himself gave example of in dealing with men. Having come not to condemn but to save, he was intransigent with evil, but merciful toward individuals. In their difficulties, may married couples always find, in the words and in the heart of a priest, the echo of the voice and the love of the Redeemer" (n. 29).

## Pope John Paul II

In his weekly audiences, in numerous talks during his travels to many nations of the world, and in his voluminous writings, Pope John Paul II spoke eloquently on every aspect of married life and love. It is not possible in this brief section of the book to do more than scratch the surface of the Holy Father's profound understanding and practical wisdom on a whole range of issues affecting family life.

Those interested in mining the depths of the Supreme Pontiff's thoughts ought to consult his many published works, and especially *Familiaris Consortio*, his 1981 apostolic exhortation on "The Role of the Christian Family in the Modern World." His frequent repetition of the Church's teaching on the immorality of contraception is staggering in both its quantity and quality.

For example, in his first visit as Pope to the United States in October 1979, His Holiness, noting that the American bishops had issued their own reaffirmation of *Humanae Vitae* in 1968, told the bishops:

> In exalting the beauty of marriage, you rightly spoke against the ideology of contraception and contraceptive acts, as did the encyclical *Humanae Vitae.* And I myself today, with the same conviction of Paul VI, ratify the teaching of his encyclical, which was put forth by my predecessor 'by virtue of the mandate entrusted to us by Christ.' "

On September 17, 1983, Pope John Paul, sounding like Pius XI in *Casti Connubii,* told a group of priests that "contraception is to be judged objectively so profoundly unlawful as never to be, for any reason, justified. To think or to say the contrary is equal to maintaining that, in human life, situations may arise in which it is lawful not to recognize God as God."

The Holy Father's stance was also reflected on March 1, 1997, when the Vatican's Pontifical Council for the Family issued a *Vade Mecum for Confessors Concerning Some Aspects of the Morality of Conjugal Life*. In that reference document for priests hearing the confessions of those engaged in contraceptive behavior, we find this unequivocal statement:

> The Church has always taught the intrinsic evil of contraception, that is, of every marital act intentionally rendered unfruitful. This teaching is to be held as definitive and irreformable. Contraception is gravely opposed to marital chastity; it is contrary to the good of the transmission of life (the procreative aspect of matrimony) and to the reciprocal self-giving of the spouses (the unitive aspect of matrimony); it harms true love and denies the sovereign role of God in the transmission of life (n. 2.4).

The document says that "in dealing with penitents on the matter of responsible procreation, the confessor should keep four aspects in mind: a) the example of the Lord, who 'is capable of reaching down to every prodigal son, to every human misery, and above all to every form of moral misery, to sin'; b) a prudent reserve in inquiring into these sins; c) help and encouragement to the penitents so that they may be able to reach sufficient repentance and accuse themselves fully of grave sins; d) advice which would inspire all, in a gradual way, to embrace the path of holiness" (n. 3.1).

That the V*ade Mecum* reflects the view of Pope John Paul is clear from the fact that 32 of the 54 footnotes to the document refer to, and sometimes quote extensively from, John Paul II.

While the Holy Father spoke on this matter literally dozens of times, his most comprehensive treatment of responsible procreation came in his 1981 apostolic exhortation *Familiaris Consortio*. Herewith some excerpts from that document on "The Role of the Christian Family in the Modern World":

**On the Constancy of This Teaching** — "In continuity with the living tradition of the ecclesial community throughout history, the recent Second Vatican Council and the Magisterium of my predecessor Paul VI, expressed above all in the encyclical *Humanae Vitae*, have handed on to our times a truly prophetic proclamation, which reaffirms and reproposes with clarity the Church's teaching and norm, always old yet always new, regarding marriage and regarding the transmission of human life.

"For this reason the Synod Fathers made the following declaration at their last assembly: 'This Sacred Synod, gathered together with the Successor of Peter in the unity of faith, firmly holds what has been set forth in the Second Vatican Council (cf. *Gaudium et Spes*, 50) and afterwards in the encyclical *Humanae Vitae* (11; cf. 9, 12), particularly that love between husband and wife must be fully human, exclusive, and open to new life' " (n. 29).

**On Government Coercion in Favor of Contraception** — "The Church is called upon to manifest anew to everyone, with clear and stronger conviction, her will to promote human life by every means and to defend it against all attacks, in whatever condition or state of development it is found.

"Thus the Church condemns as a grave offense against human dignity and justice all those activities of governments or other public authorities which attempt to limit in any way the freedom of couples in deciding about children. Consequently, any violence applied by such authorities in favor of contraception or, still worse, of sterilization and procured abortion, must be altogether condemned and forcefully rejected.

"Likewise to be denounced as gravely unjust are cases where, in international relations, economic help given for the advancement of peoples is made conditional on programs of contraception, sterilization, and procured abortion" (n. 30).

**On the Necessity of Holiness and Sacrifice** — "In God's plan, all husbands and wives are called in marriage to holiness, and this lofty vocation is fulfilled to the extent that the human person is able to respond to God's command with serene confidence in God's grace and in his or her own will. On the same lines, it is part of the Church's pedagogy that husbands and wives should first recognize clearly the teaching of *Humanae Vitae* as indicating the norm for the exercise of their sexuality, and that they should endeavor to establish the conditions necessary for observing that norm.

"As the Synod noted, this pedagogy embraces the whole of married life. Accordingly, the function of transmitting life must be integrated into the overall mission of Christian life as a whole, which without the Cross cannot reach the Resurrection. In such a context it is understandable that sacrifice cannot be removed from family life, but must in fact be wholeheartedly accepted if the love between husband and wife is to be deepened and become a source of intimate joy" (n. 34).

## Connection Between Contraception and Abortion

Before leaving the writings of Pope John Paul, we want to refer to a section of *Evangelium Vitae*, his 1995 encyclical on "The Gospel of Life." While that document deals primarily with the taking of innocent human life, the Holy Father spent some time establishing the nexus between contraception and abortion. Supporters of contraception deny such a link, but John Paul's argument is very persuasive.

"It is frequently asserted," the Holy Father said, "that contraception, if made safe and available to all, is the most effective remedy against abortion. The Catholic Church is then accused of actually promoting abortion because she obstinately continues to teach the moral unlawfulness of contraception. When looked at carefully, this objection is clearly unfounded. It may be that many people use contraception with a view to excluding the subsequent temptation of abortion. But the negative values inherent in the 'contraceptive mentality' — which is very different from responsible parenthood lived in respect for the full truth of the conjugal act — are such that they in fact strengthen this temptation when an unwanted life is conceived."

Indeed, the Holy Father continued, "the pro-abortion culture is especially strong precisely where the Church's teaching on contraception is rejected. Certainly, from the moral point of view, contraception and abortion are specifically different evils: the former contradicts the full truth of the sexual act as the proper expression of conjugal love, while the latter destroys the life of a human being; the former is opposed to the virtue of chastity in marriage, the latter is opposed to the virtue of justice and directly violates the divine commandment 'You shall not kill.' "

Despite these differences, however, the Pontiff said that "contraception and abortion are often closely connected, as fruits of the same tree. It is true that in many cases contraception and even abortion are practiced under the pressure of real-life difficulties, which nonetheless can never exonerate from striving to observe God's law fully. Still, in very many other instances such practices are rooted in a hedonistic mentality unwilling to accept responsibility in matters of sexuality, and they imply a self-centered concept of freedom, which regards procreation as an obstacle to personal fulfillment. The life which could result from a sexual encounter thus becomes an enemy to be avoided at all costs, and abortion becomes the only possible decisive response to failed contraception."

John Paul concluded this section of *Evangelium Vitae* by stating that "the close connection which exists in mentality between the practice of contraception and that of abortion is becoming increasingly obvious. It is being demonstrated in an alarming way by the development of chemical products, intrauterine devices, and vaccines which, distributed with the same ease as contraceptives, really act as abortifacients in the very early stages of the development of the life of the new human being" (n. 13).

## Catechism of the Catholic Church

In a section entitled "The Fecundity of Marriage," the *Catechism of the Catholic Church* reaffirmed the constant teaching of the Church against artificial means of contraception. After saying that Natural Family Planning methods of birth regulation were in conformity with Church teaching, the *Catechism*, quoting from *Humanae Vitae*, said that "these methods respect the bodies of the spouses, encourage tenderness between them, and favor the education of an authentic freedom. In contrast, 'every action which, whether in anticipation of the conjugal act, or in its accomplishment, or in the development of its natural consequences, proposes, whether as an end or as a means, to render procreation impossible' is intrinsically evil" (n. 2370).

Quoting next from *Familiaris Consortio*, the *Catechism* said:

> Thus the innate language that expresses the total reciprocal self-giving of husband and wife is overlaid, through contraception, by an objectively contradictory language, namely, that

of not giving oneself totally to the other. This leads not only to a positive refusal to be open to life but also to a falsification of the inner truth of conjugal love, which is called upon to give itself in personal totality .... The difference, both anthropological and moral, between contraception and recourse to the rhythm of the cycle ... involves in the final analysis two irreconcilable concepts of the human person and of human sexuality (*Ibid.*).

## What Is Contraception?

**Contraception, as we have seen, is any direct, positive frustration of any phase in the process of conception before, during, or after a voluntary act of intercourse.** In this definition, the word "contraception" is used in a moral sense, not merely in a biological sense. "Direct" distinguishes sinful frustration from indirect frustration, sometimes permitted by the principle of the twofold or double effect, as in the case of a diseased uterus. "Positive" distinguishes contraception from the use of Natural Family Planning, and the word "voluntary" excludes rape. However, "voluntary" must be taken literally; an act performed reluctantly is still voluntary.

In speaking of contraception, the terms "Onanism," "birth control," and "planned parenthood" are frequently used. However, one must judge from the particular context whether such terms are understood as synonyms for immoral contraception. If a procedure, device, or medication causes abortion — as does the Pill (some of the time), the intrauterine device (IUD), or the drug RU-486 — then it is not contraception and should be judged according to the moral principles governing abortion.

## Means of Contraception

When we talk about artificial means of contraception, we are talking about a variety of things:

**Coitus interruptus** — This is withdrawal by the male during sexual intercourse. It is also known as Onanism and is mentioned in the Bible as deserving of death.

**Barrier Methods** — These devices, which are designed to prevent the sperm from reaching the egg, include male and female condoms, diaphragms, vaginal sponges, and cervical caps. Some would include the intrauterine device in this category, but since the IUD is designed to render the wall of the uterus hostile to a newly created human life and cause an early abortion, it is not a contraceptive but an abortifacient.

**Chemical Methods** — Also designed to block the sperm from fertilizing the egg, these include spermicidal foams, jellies, creams, and douches. Their use to prevent conception is immoral. A water douche used solely for hygenic reasons would not be sinful, but one used immediately after intercourse with contraceptive intent would be sinful, regardless of its effectiveness as a contraceptive.

**Pharmacological Methods** — These include Norplant devices, Depo-Provera injections, and the "Pill" (estrogen with progestin), or their equivalent, all of which have abortifacient as well as contraceptive effects, and RU-486, or its equivalent under whatever name, which causes the developing child to be aborted. The birth control Pill acts in three major ways: (1) It usually prevents the release of a new egg from the ovaries. (2) It thickens the mucus in the reproductive tract, thus making it more difficult for the sperm to reach the egg. (3) If the first two effects do not occur, and a new human life is conceived, the Pill causes the wall of the uterus to resist implantation and leads to the death of the tiny embryo.

Although referred to by drug firms and in medical books, it is rarely realized by the public that there are many potentially dangerous side effects or "adverse reactions" associated with the infusion of this powerful drug into the body. These side effects include heart and blood abnormalities, gastro-intestinal problems, eye problems, effects on gall bladder and liver, unanticipated bleeding in various organs, and many more complications which cannot be ignored (cf. *Nursing Drug Handbook*). The dictum that violations of the natural law will result not only in adverse supernatural consequences, but in natural ones as well, gives pause for thought.

RU-486, sometimes euphemistically referred to as a "post-coital contraceptive," is in reality an abortion pill that blocks the action of progesterone, the naturally occurring hormone which is produced in pregnancy to maintain the rich nutrient lining of the uterus. It prevents the uterus from getting the chemical "message" to maintain the pregnancy, causing the uterine lining to break down and cut off the developing child from his supply of food, fluids, and oxygen. The baby shrivels and finally suffocates or starves to death. A prostaglandin given about two days later stimulates uterine contractions to expel the unborn child.

Obviously, if the use of powerful drugs to prevent conception is immoral, then use of them to kill a child already conceived is even more evil. And, as the years go by, more evidence is piling up about the physical and emotional complications experienced by women who have taken these drugs for contraceptive purposes.

## A Necessary Moral Distinction

At this point, we should note that there is a moral distinction between those procedures which constitute a perversion of the natural act of intercourse, such as withdrawal or the use of barrier methods, and those which affect the functioning of the procreative organs, such as drugs which inhibit ovulation. The performance of the procreative act in an unnatural manner is intrinsically evil and is not morally allowable for any reason.

On the other hand, some surgical or pharmacological procedures that affect the procreative faculties are morally indifferent in themselves and therefore require at times application of the principle of the twofold effect. When this principle is applicable, then the intention of the responsible party enters into the determination of the morality of the act. Of course, when the act itself is intrinsically evil, then the act is always wrong and the intention of the person is not an issue.

For example, taking medication which inhibits ovulation (and therefore conception) is not in itself contrary to nature and intrinsically immoral. Therefore, such an action cannot be automatically condemned on the basis of intrinsic immorality. What determines the morality in this case is the purpose of the act.

Thus, if a woman takes a drug for the direct and exclusive purpose of preventing conception, she commits a serious sin. However, if she takes the drug for the direct purpose of curing or alleviating a serious pathological condition, such as endometriosis or uterine bleeding, no sin is committed, even though sterility may also result from the treatment. It would also be morally permissible to take a medication in order to achieve menstrual regularity, even though temporary sterility would result.

This is an application of the double-effect principle. It should be noted, however, that if it is possible to effect a cure without interfering with conception, then the principle of the double effect could not be applied. The same principles would hold true in any parallel situations involving males.

In certain cases of apparent sterility, some physicians have expressed the belief that the probability of conception is increased

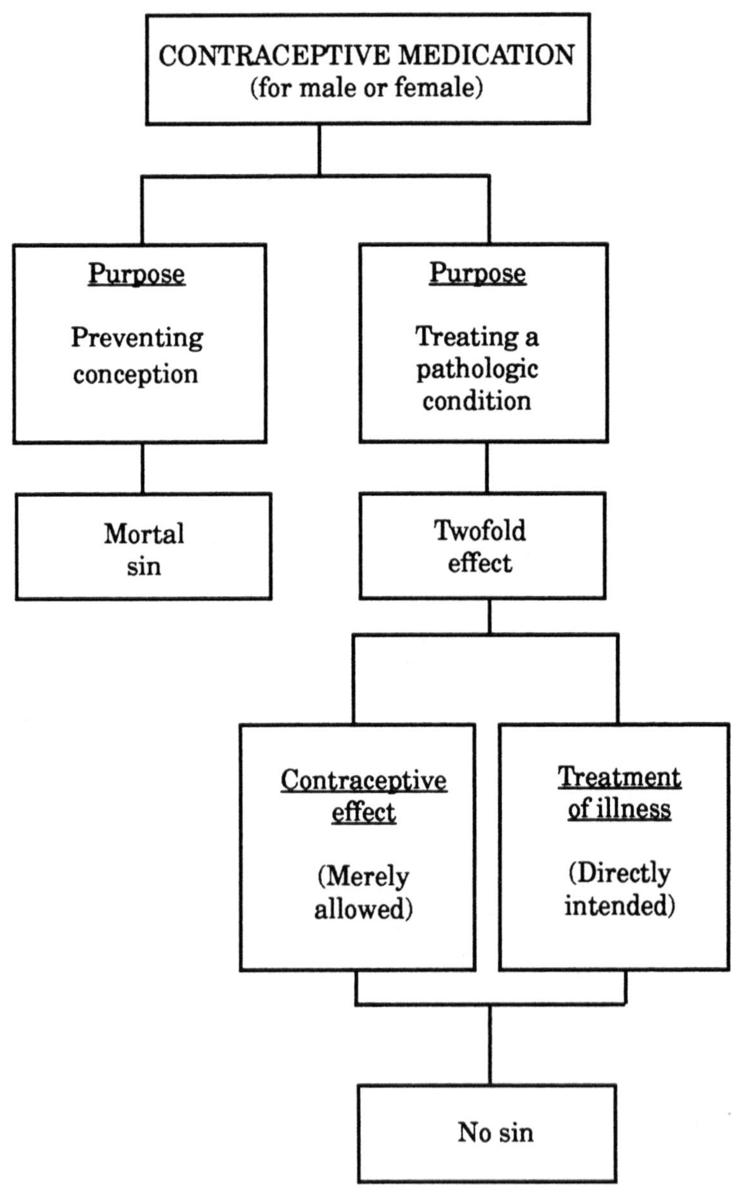


*The Morality of Contraceptive Medication*

if ovulation is suppressed for a time. This procedure (ovulation rebound) is moral under the principle of totality since one function of the body is temporarily suppressed for the general good of the whole body.

In other words, medication may be taken for the purpose of achieving fertility, even though ovulation is impeded as a means to a good end. The means used is not an evil one, but an indifferent one, and its morality is therefore determined by its purpose. Of course, this moral conclusion is based on the supposition that harmful side effects from the medication are precluded.

## Surgical Means

Surgical means of contraception, i.e., operations having sterilization as their direct purpose (vasectomy for males and tubal ligation for females), are immoral and will be treated at length in chapter nine.

## Moral Methods of Birth Regulation

In the course of married life, there can be valid reasons why the conception of a child may be inadvisable. For example, severe financial difficulties, lack of adequate housing, temporary illness of husband or wife, or certain physical or mental afflictions. Since we have already established that the use of contraception is not allowable for any reason or in any situation, then what are married couples to do when faced with the problems just mentioned? There are only two natural options: total abstinence from intercourse or periodic abstinence during those sterile times when no egg is present and the woman cannot conceive a child.

Because we live in an age when people are encouraged to satisfy all their desires and to deny themselves nothing, the thought of abstaining from sex, even for brief periods of time, strikes some people as an impossible task. A difficult task, yes, but not impossible. After all, husbands and wives have to forego sexual relations before and after the birth of a baby, or in times of sickness, or when one spouse is away on a trip.

So abstinence is not impossible for couples who have serious reasons for postponing a pregnancy and who ask God for his help through prayer and the sacraments. God never obliges us to do the impossible, but he does oblige married couples to abstain in certain circumstances. Therefore, abstinence is possible. Here is how the Council of Trent phrased it:

God does not ask the impossible, but by his commands instructs you to do what you are able, to pray for what you are not able that he may help you.

## Natural Family Planning

Before discussing the morality of Natural Family Planning (NFP), and how it is different from contraception, we need to point out that we are not talking about the old and unreliable calendar rhythm method where a woman pretty much guessed at what days during her menstrual cycle that she would be infertile. That method resulted in many more pregnancies than its practitioners had planned.

When we talk about NFP today, we are referring to a scientific method involving systematic observation of a woman's bodily signs of fertility and infertility through daily changes in body temperature and cervical mucus. All of these signs are carefully charted and studied to determine a woman's fertile period. And by the way, we should mention that NFP can be used to achieve pregnancy, as well as to avoid it.

It is not the purpose of this book to explain how NFP works; a comprehensive and readable explanation has been provided by John and Sheila Kippley in their book *The Art of Natural Family Planning*. The book is available through the Couple to Couple League in Cincinnati, Ohio, which the Kippleys founded in 1971 to help couples build happy marriages through NFP.

The method they have taught to thousands of married couples is safe, healthy, inexpensive, and highly effective. It has also strengthened marriages because it encourages spouses to love each other through communication and self-control during times of abstinence. It requires the loving cooperation of both husband and wife, unlike contraceptive methods that usually put all the burden on the woman and require her to jeopardize her health by taking powerful drugs or using dangerous devices.

If husband and wife are able to control their natural drives and practice self-denial through periodic continence, Pope John Paul told an audience in Rome on August 28, 1984, "self-discipline of this kind is a shining witness to the chastity of husband and wife and, so far from being a hindrance to their love of one another, transforms it by giving it a more truly human character ... enabling husband and wife to develop to the full their personalities."

The licitness of abstinence during the fertile times is not something new. Pope Pius XI, in *Casti Connubii*, said:

> Nor are those considered as acting against nature who in the married state use their right in the proper manner, although on account of natural reasons either of time or of certain defects, new life cannot be brought forth. For in matrimony as well as in the use of the matrimonial rights there are also secondary ends, such as mutual aid, the cultivating of mutual love, and the quieting of concupiscence which husband and wife are not forbidden to consider as long as they are subordinated to the primary end and so long as the intrinsic nature of the act is preserved (n. 59).

Pope Pius XII repeated this caution in his address to Italian midwives in 1951, Pope Paul VI echoed his predecessors in section 16 of *Humanae Vitae*, Pope John Paul II reaffirmed the teaching in section 32 of *Familiaris Consortio*, and the *Catechism of the Catholic Church* stated that "periodic continence, that is, methods of birth regulation based on self-observation and the use of the infertile periods, is in conformity with the objective criteria of morality" (n. 2370).

So Natural Family Planning is a morally permissible way of spacing out births and engaging in responsible parenthood. Remember, though, that the couple must have what Pope Paul called "serious motives" to practice NFP. A priest or moral theologian who is loyal to the Magisterium of the Church would be the proper judge of what constitutes a serious motive in a particular case.

Furthermore, the mutual consent of both spouses is necessary. Marital relations may not normally be refused by one party, except for a serious reason. And one could not use this method if its use would cause the other party to sin, either alone or with a third party. If, however, certain extraordinary circumstances are present, such as the possibility of the wife's death should she become pregnant or true serious financial difficulties, then she would have the right to demand that her husband practice NFP.

In summary, Natural Family Planning may be used only (1) for serious reasons, (2) with mutual consent, and (3) if the danger of sin is excluded.

## Differences Between NFP and Contraception

Some people contend that Natural Family Planning and contraception are essentially the same thing since both seek to avoid pregnancy. Both methods do indeed aim to prevent pregnancy, but morally they are not the same. Contraception involves taking direct and deliberate steps before, during, or after marital intercourse to avoid pregnancy. NFP involves no marital act at all. In other words, contraception means doing something, while NFP means doing nothing.

There's a big difference, morally speaking, between acting against something and not acting against it. In the case of a terminal cancer patient, for example, it would be morally wrong to kill the patient with a drug injection, but it would not be wrong to forgo an operation that at best might only keep the patient alive for a short time.

A couple who for serious reasons seeks to practice responsible parenthood can abstain from marital relations without harboring a hostile attitude toward human life. They are not attacking life at its very beginning through chemical or mechanical means, but are rather allowing every marital act to remain open to new life.

Couples who resort to contraception, Pope John Paul said in *Familiaris Consortio*, "act as 'arbiters' of the divine plan and they 'manipulate' and degrade human sexuality — and with it themselves and their married partner — by altering its value of 'total' self-giving. Thus the innate language that expresses the total reciprocal self-giving of husband and wife is overlaid, through contraception, by an objectively contradictory language, namely, that of not giving oneself totally to the other" (n. 32).

Those who practice NFP, on the other hand, act "as 'ministers' of God's plan and they 'benefit from' their sexuality according to the original dynamism of 'total' self-giving, without manipulation or alteration," the Holy Father said. He said that the experience of many couples and data provided by the different human sciences show that the difference between contraception and recourse to the rhythm of the cycle "is much wider and deeper than is usually thought, one which involves in the final analysis two irreconcilable concepts of the human person and of human sexuality."

The Pope went on to say that "the choice of the natural rhythms involves accepting the cycle of the person, that is the woman, and thereby accepting dialogue, reciprocal respect, shared responsibility, and self-control. To accept the cycle and to enter into dialogue means to recognize both the spiritual and the corporal character of conjugal communion, and to live personal love with its requirement of fidelity."

He said that "in this context the couple comes to experience how conjugal communion is enriched with those values of tenderness and affection which constitute the inner soul of human sexuality, in its physical dimension also. In this way sexuality is respected and promoted in its truly and fully human dimension, and is never 'used' as an 'object' that, by breaking the personal unity of soul and body, strikes at God's creation itself at the level of the deepest interaction of nature and person" (n. 32).

## Manipulating Human Life

We have thus far in this chapter been talking of ways that allow couples to engage in sex without reproduction. Now we will discuss technologies that allow persons to achieve reproduction without sex. This slide down the slippery slope into what Aldous Huxley called a "Brave New World" continues today as scientists seek new and more bizarre ways of manipulating the origins of human life. These techniques include cloning, in vitro fertilization, surrogate motherhood, artificial insemination, sterility testing, and fertility drugs.

The Church, as always, sets forth the principles by which Catholics can judge these techniques. One of the most important sources of those principles is the 1987 document of the Sacred Congregation for the Doctrine of the Faith entitled "Instruction on Respect for Human Life in Its Origin and on the Dignity of Procreation" (*Donum Vitae)*.

Before taking up the scientific interventions into human procreation, the document made clear that science and technology "must be at the service of the human person, of his inalienable rights and his true and integral good according to the design and will of God. The rapid development of technological discoveries gives greater urgency to this need to respect the criteria just mentioned: science without conscience can only lead to man's ruin" (Introduction, 1).

The transmission of plant and animal life is one thing, said *Donum Vitae*, but "the transmission of human life has a special character of its own which derives from the special nature of the human person. 'The transmission of human life is entrusted by nature to a personal and conscious act and as such is subject to the all-holy laws of God: immutable and inviolable laws which must be recognized and observed. For this reason, one cannot use means and follow methods which could be licit in the transmisison of the life of plants and animals' " (Introduction, 4).

Advances in technology have made it possible to procreate apart from sexual relations, the document said, but insisted that "what is technically possible is not for that very reason morally admissible" (*Ibid.*). It explained why this is so in the following passage:

> From the moment of conception, the life of every human being is to be respected in an absolute way because man is the only creature on earth that God has "wished for himself," and the spiritual soul of each man is "immediately created" by God; his whole being bears the image of the Creator. Human life is sacred because from its beginning it involves "the creative action of God," and it remains forever in a special relationship with the Creator, who is its sole end. God alone is the Lord of life from its beginning until its end; no one can, in any circumstance, claim for himself the right to destroy an innocent human being.
>
> Human procreation requires on the part of the spouses responsible collaboration with the fruitful love of God; the gift of human life must be actualized in marriage through the specific and exclusive acts of husband and wife, in accordance with the laws inscribed in their persons and in their union (Introduction, 5).

## Cloning

Cloning involves taking the DNA from a mature, fully differentiated adult cell and placing it into an unfertilized egg cell from which the nucleus has been removed and fusing them together by an electrical stimulation. The new cell begins to divide and grow and produces, as in the case of the sheep cloned in Scotland in 1997, a new organism. While such a process can be justified in animals, provided that the research is directed toward good purposes, is carried out with concern for the protection of the animal and the integrity of various species, and is performed only under strict ethical guidelines, it can never be justified in the replication of human beings. In the words of *Donum Vitae*:

> Attempts or hypotheses for obtaining a human being without any connection with sexuality through "twin fission," cloning, or parthogenesis are to be considered contrary to the moral law since they are in opposition to the dignity both of human procreation and of the conjugal union (Part I, 6).

What are some of the reasons for opposing the cloning of human beings? In testimony before a New York State Senate Committee on March 13, 1997, John Cardinal O'Connor, Archbishop of New York, listed some important objections to cloning:

First, it is a drastic invasion of human parenthood. A clone technically has no human parents, not by accident, but by design. This does disrespect both to the dignity of human procreation and the dignity of the conjugal union (marriage). Contrary to the right of every human person to be conceived and born within marriage and from marriage, the clone is reduced to the level of a product made rather than a person begotten...

To reduce human procreation to no more, no better, or no different than plant or animal replication — without human parenthood — is to remove the *humanum* from human parents and the human child. (The potential psychological consequences, proximate and remote, for both clone and cloner are simply unknown. But with humans it is not enough not to know we do harm; with humans we must know that we cause no harm. The first canon of medical ethics remains: *primum non nocere*! First, do no harm!).

A second basic objection to human cloning is on the level of human wisdom. Take a sober look at our external environment. Consider the man-made damage done to our natural external environment, some foreseen, much unforeseen. Is any serious person that sanguine about the state of our external environment that he or she is positively anxious now to "engineer" our internal human evolution? Do we have the wisdom?

The Scottish-cloned sheep, Dolly, came into being on the 300th attempt. The first 277 attempts did not even fuse. From 278 to 299 they did fuse but, misguided, misshaped, grew a bit and essentially fell apart. Switch focus to human beings. No. 1 try is blue-eyed. Wrong color. Only brown is acceptable. Oops, I wanted a boy. Get rid of this girl. Etc., etc., etc. How many human beings are destroyed before the ideal is achieved? Ideal according to whose standards? Do we throw human beings away like paper napkins?...

At least in human procreation there is a natural community (mother and father) to receive new life. In human cloning, it is not truly the "parent(s)" who decides but the technicians who determine which "quality types" qualify for membership in the human community. Is this limited to the married? Is it limited to one sex or the other? Is there a controllable agenda to preclude one sex or the other?

> The third basic objection to human cloning includes social and ethical questions. Cloning is not now and never will be a poor people's campaign. Could it be or become an entitlement requiring public subsidy? This is a most undesirable shift because it replaces ethical categories with manufacturing imperatives. The act of human cloning itself cures no pathology. Thus, we are not doctoring the patient but doctoring the race.
>
> There remains a profound ethical difference between "having a child" and "making a child." A child begotten can always be seen as a gift, whereas a child made or manufactured can always be seen as a thing — a product for use, not to be respected for what he/she is, but prized for what it can do, have, or be used for. That is no way to treat or value a human being.
>
> In this shift, the scientific canons of efficiency replace the ethics of life. That is a giant societal step in the wrong direction. It is ironic that now, near the close of the 20th century, a century that spent great time and effort to have sex without babies, now some want to have babies without sex (*Origins*, April 10, 1997, p. 683).

Cardinal O'Connor was echoed on June 24, 1997, when the Pontifical Academy for Life issued a condemnation of human cloning, saying that "stopping the human cloning project is a moral task that should be translated into cultural, social, and legislative terms." The Pontifical Academy said that the process would violate the basic human rights of equal dignity and nondiscrimination, replace human reproduction with "the logic of industrial production," promote a "radical exploitation" of women, and destroy natural family relationships that have always existed.

## In Vitro Fertilization

Another aspect of genetic manipulation is the production of babies in the laboratory through a process known as in vitro fertilization (IVF) and embryo transfer (ET). This involves bringing together in a dish containing a nutrient solution (hence the phrase "test-tube baby") an egg cell from a woman and a sperm cell from a man. Once fertilization occurs, the tiny human embryo is transferred into a woman's uterus and is expected to develop throughout a normal pregnancy, although studies have shown the success rate of babies born via this method to be about 25 percent. The first successful IVF procedure took place in England in 1978 and, since then, many thousands of babies have been delivered this way.

While the successful procedures get a great deal of publicity, less well known are the negative aspects of IVF, which include experimentation on and destruction of human embryos, freezing of embryos for later implantation, genetic manipulation of human gametes with animals, and "surrogate motherhood," whereby certain women "rent out" their wombs to carry children for other women who are either unable or unwilling to experience pregnancy themselves.

Speaking at a symposium on *Evangelium Vitae* and the law on May 24, 1996, Pope John Paul II urged scientists to halt the production of human embryos. "The human embryo has basic rights," the Holy Father said, adding that "I consider it my duty once again to assert these inviolable rights of the human being from his conception on behalf of all the embryos which are often subjected to freezing (cryopreservation), in many cases becoming an object of sheer experimentation or, worse, destined to be programmed in destruction backed by law."

The Pontiff issued an "appeal to the conscience of the world's scientific authorities, and in particular to doctors, that the production of human embryos be halted, taking into account that there seems to be no morally licit solution regarding the human destiny of the thousands and thousands of 'frozen' embryos which are and remain the subjects of essential rights and should therefore be protected by law as human persons."

He also called on "all jurists to work so that states and international institutions will legally recognize the natural rights of the very origin of human life and will likewise defend the inalienable rights which these thousands of 'frozen' embryos have intrinsically acquired from the moment of fertilization. Government leaders themselves cannot shirk this duty, if the value of democracy, which is rooted in recognizing the inviolable rights of every human individual, is to be safeguarded at its very origins."

This solution to the fertility problems faced by increasing numbers of couples has been condemned by the Church primarily because it undermines the unitive (love-giving) and procreative (life-giving) purposes of the marital union. The IVF/ET procedure enlists many people. A male and female produce the sperm and ovum, someone else collects both, others prepare them for fertilization, and someone transfers the resulting embryo to the woman. Instead of a mutual self-giving of spouses, there is only a technical process. In addition, the sperm is usually obtained by the immoral means of masturbation.

The desire for a child, laudable though that is, is not enough to make IVF a morally permissible action, said *Donum Vitae*, since, "in the circumstances in which it is regularly practiced, IVF and ET involves the destruction of human beings, which is something contrary to the doctrine of the illicitness of abortion previously mentioned. But even in a situation in which every precaution were taken to avoid the death of human embryos, homologous [using the husband's sperm] IVF and ET dissociates from the conjugal act the actions which are directed to human fertilization" (Part II, 5).

Further, said *Donum Vitae*, "IVF and ET is brought about outside the bodies of the couple through actions of third parties whose competence and technical activity determine the success of the procedure. Such fertilization entrusts the life and identity of the embryo into the power of doctors and biologists and establishes the domination of technology over the origin and destiny of the human person. Such a relationship of domination is in itself contrary to the dignity and equality that must be common to parents and children" (*Ibid.*).

These reasons, the document explained, "enable us to understand why the act of conjugal love is considered the only setting worthy of human procreation. For the same reasons, the so-called 'simple case,' i.e., a homologous IVF and ET procedure that is free of any compromise with the abortive practice of destroying embryos and with masturbation, remains a technique which is morally illicit because it deprives human procreation of the dignity which is proper and connatural to it" (*Ibid.*).

It is also important to note the Congregation's statement a few sentences later, namely, that while the Church cannot approve conception of a child via in vitro fertilization, nevertheless "every child which comes into the world must in any case be accepted as a living gift of the divine Goodness and must be brought up with love" (*Ibid.*).

## Surrogate Motherhood

Just when you thought that IVF was pushing the moral and biological envelope, along came surrogate motherhood where some women were willing, usually for money, to carry another woman's child until birth. This arrangement became even more complicated when a few surrogate mothers refused to give up the babies they had been carrying, and courts had to settle the issue. As far as the licitness of this process is concerned, *Donum Vitae* also settled the morality of the issue for Catholics:

> Is "surrogate" motherhood morally licit? No, for the same reasons which lead one to reject heterologous [using the sperm or egg from a third party] artificial fertilization: for it is contrary to the unity of marriage and to the dignity of the procreation of the human person.
>
> Surrogate motherhood represents an objective failure to meet the obligations of maternal love, of conjugal fidelity, and of responsible motherhood; it offends the dignity and the right of the child to be conceived, carried in the womb, brought into the world, and brought up by his own parents; it sets up, to the detriment of families, a division between the physical, psychological, and moral elements which constitute those families (Part II, A, 3).

The *Catechism of the Catholic Church* is even more forceful:

> Techniques that entail the dissociation of husband and wife, by the intrusion of a person other than the couple (donation of sperm or ovum, surrogate uterus), are gravely immoral. These techniques (heterologous artificial insemination and fertilization) infringe the child's right to be born of a father and mother known to him and bound to each other by marriage. They betray the spouses' 'right to become a father and a mother only through each other' " (n. 2376).

## Artificial Insemination

While we have already referred briefly to artificial insemination, let us take an overall look at this subject. We can start by saying that **artificial insemination is any attempt to fertilize a female by a means which is a substitute for natural intercourse**. It cannot be considered exclusively from a biological and medical viewpoint; it is first and foremost a moral matter. So we will also discuss, in light of fast-moving technological advances, the moral implications of various kinds of artificial insemination.

As is so often the case in medical/moral issues, Pope Pius XII long ago gave clear guidance on this and related topics. Addressing the Second World Congress on Fertility and Sterility on May 19, 1956, the Holy Father stated: "Artificial insemination violates the natural law and is illicit and immoral."

His concern for the natural law, and for the basic concept of marriage and sexuality, was echoed nearly three decades later by Pope John Paul, who told a general audience on August 22, 1984, that "the conjugal act 'signifies' not only love, but also potential fecundity and therefore it cannot be deprived of its full and adequate significance by artificial means. In the conjugal act, it is not licit to separate the unitive aspect from the procreative aspect because both the one and the other pertain to the intimate truth of the conjugal act: the one is activated together with the other and in a certain sense the one by means of the other."

Herewith a brief survey of the different categories of artificial insemination:

**Artificial insemination between the married** — With regard to the lawfulness of artificial insemination in marriage, when fertilization is impossible in the usual way, it is sufficient to recall the principles of the natural law, which state that artificial insemination will not render a marriage valid between persons who are unfit to contract marriage because of the impediment of impotency. Impotency is the inability to perform the marriage act.

It is lawful to use scientific methods to promote fertilization once natural intercourse has taken place. This is sometimes referred to as "assisted insemination" to stress the connection with a natural act of marriage. It is never lawful for any reason to obtain sperm by means of masturbation. The seed can lawfully be obtained by collecting semen with a perforated Silastic sheath that is used during marital intercourse.

There are also procedures in which an ovum that cannot get through a blocked fallopian tube can be transferred to a lower position in the tube or in the womb to make fertilization possible. If a procedure can be considered "assisted natural insemination," and if it does not involve procuring the sperm by methods that Pius XII referred to as "acts contrary to nature," then the Holy Father said on November 26, 1951, that he would not rule out "the use of certain artificial means designed only to facilitate the natural act or to enable that act, performed in a normal manner, to attain its end."

**Artificial insemination outside marriage** — Artificial insemination outside marriage is condemned as immoral. A child conceived in this fashion is, by this fact alone, illegitimate. The natural law dictates that the procreation of new life may only be the fruit of marriage since marriage alone safeguards the dignity of husband and wife, and marriage alone provides for the proper upbringing of the child.

**Artificial insemination by a third party** — Artificial insemination in marriage with the use of sperm or ovum from a third person, even with the consent of the husband or wife, is more immoral than artificial insemination outside marriage because it is substantially adultery. Only marriage partners have mutual rights over their bodies for the procreation of a new life, and these rights are exclusive, non-transferable, and inalienable. Moreover, the husband and wife have no moral right to give anyone permission to involve their spouse in artificial insemination.

Nature imposes on whoever gives life to an infant the task of its preservation and education. However, there is no such moral or juridical bond between marriage partners and a child that is the fruit of insemination by a donor. This is particularly true in the case of children conceived via in vitro fertilization.

Some have argued that a sperm donor is like a person who donates blood. But there is no parallel. Insemination by a donor involves the generation of a new human person, but the biological father, who is usually paid for his services, is expected to abandon a human relationship with his offspring. Again, we refer to *Donum Vitae* for guidelines concerning the morality of this process:

> Respect for the unity of marriage and for conjugal fidelity demands that the child be conceived in marriage; the bond existing between husband and wife accords the spouses, in an objective and inalienable manner, the exclusive right to become father and mother solely through each other. Recourse to the gametes of a third person, in order to have sperm or ovum available, constitutes a violation of the reciprocal commitment of the spouses and a grave lack in regard to that essential property of marriage which is its unity.

> Heterologous artificial fertilization violates the rights of the child; it deprives him of his filial relationship with his parental origins and can hinder the maturing of his personal identity. Furthermore, it offends the common vocation of the spouses who are called to fatherhood and motherhood: it objectively deprives conjugal fruitfulness of its unity and integ-

rity; it brings about and manifests a rupture between genetic parenthood, gestational parenthood, and responsibility for upbringing. Such damage to the personal relationships within the family has repercussions on civil society: what threatens the unity and stability of the family is a source of dissension, disorder, and injustice in the whole of social life.

These reasons lead to a negative moral judgment concerning heterologous artificial fertilization: consequently, fertilization of a married woman with the sperm of a donor different from her husband and fertilization with the husband's sperm of an ovum not coming from his wife are morally illicit. Furthermore, the artificial fertilization of a woman who is unmarried or a widow, whoever the donor may be, cannot be morally justified (Part II, 2).

## Prenatal Testing

When there is the suspicion that a pregnant woman may be carrying a child with a birth defect, such as Down's Syndrome or Tay-Sach's Disease, doctors will frequently recommend a procedure known as amniocentesis. It involves withdrawing a small amount of fluid from the baby's amniotic sac through a needle inserted into the mother's abdomen and uterine wall. The cells in the fluid are examined and, if there appears to be a serious problem, "termination of pregnancy," a euphemism for abortion, is usually recommended.

Newer methods of diagnosing handicapped babies before birth, such as chorionic villi biopsy, also lead to killing the baby to "cure" the disease.

Amniocentesis tests done in the last three months of pregnancy are much safer for the baby and can help save the lives of mother and baby by identifying such problems as Rh disease, diabetes, and fetal lung immaturity. But when they are done in the second three months, a period when no fetal conditions can be treated, says Dr. J.C. Willke, they are nothing more than "search and destroy" missions (*Abortion: Questions and Answers*, p. 272).

Prenatal diagnosis, if carried out to identify the medical treatment which may be needed by the child in the womb, is morally permissible. But when it becomes a procedure that leads to abortion, it is immoral (cf. *Evangelium Vitae*, n. 14). Moral theologian William E. May, in his book *Human Existence, Medicine and Ethics*, summarizes Catholic thought on amniocentesis:

> Most of those who advocate this procedure are not cold, ruthless, insensitive persons. They are motivated by compassion for people, for the suffering that human beings experience when genetically crippled children are born. They want to alleviate human misery. Through amniocentesis, followed by abortion, they seek to minimize suffering....
>
> However, in their desire to alleviate suffering, they have adopted a consequentialistic ethics that justifies human activities in terms of good results .... This pragmatic way of approaching moral issues can justify anything on the grounds that the end justifies the means .... There are strong moral arguments against screening with a view to abortion.

Another prenatal test is ultrasound, a non-invasive procedure used to visualize the baby in utero. It has become very common today in the management of pregnancy. A crystal transducer emitting sound waves is guided over the mother's pelvis and an image (sonogram) is projected on a monitor. This method can confirm a pregnancy as early as the sixth week of gestation, and it can detect multiple babies and some congenital abnormalities. It is most useful late in pregnancy in determining the size, position, development, and sex of the baby, as well as the date of delivery.

Sadly, this valuable information is sometimes used for determining if the pregnancy will be allowed to go full term or whether the child should be aborted because the little one is the wrong sex or might present health problems after birth. Ultrasound is a safe medical procedure and is morally acceptable provided that it is not used to screen for possible abortions. We turn again to *Donum Vitae* for the Church's official position:

> Is prenatal diagnosis morally licit? If prenatal diagnosis respects the life and integrity of the embryo and the human fetus and is directed towards its safeguarding or healing as an individual, then the answer is affirmative. For prenatal diagnosis makes it possible to know the condition of the embryo and of the fetus when still in the mother's womb. It permits, or makes it possible to anticipate earlier and more effectively, certain therapeutic, medical, or surgical procedures.
>
> Such diagnosis is permissible, with the consent of the parents after they have been adequately informed, if the methods employed safeguard the life and integrity of the embryo and the

mother, without subjecting them to disproportionate risks. But this diagnosis is gravely opposed to the moral law when it is done with the thought of possibly inducing an abortion depending upon the results: a diagnosis which shows the existence of a malformation or a hereditary illness must not be the equivalent of a death sentence. Thus a woman would be committing a gravely illicit act if she were to request such a diagnosis with the deliberate intention of having an abortion should the results confirm the existence of a malformation or abnormality (Part I, 2).

## Sterility Testing

Sterility is the inability to reproduce, and a considerable number of marriages today are childless because of sterility. Correction of this problem is of great importance and increasing numbers of couples are imploring medical assistance. In seeking a solution to sterility, however, one must not engage in immoral acts, such as masturbation for a man to obtain semen for testing. But semen samples can be obtained, as noted earlier, through the use of a perforated Silastic sheath during marital intercourse.

Another moral issue involves the taking of fertility drugs, which can lead to multiple births and possible "pregnancy reduction" (abortion) to reduce the number of children born. What moral guidelines should be considered before going this route? Peter J. Cataldo, Ph.D., of the Pope John Center for the Study of Ethics in Health Care in Braintree, Massachusetts, offers this advice:

> Given that "pregnancy reduction" is ethically out of the question, the use of these drugs seems to be morally permissible, with certain qualifications, to overcome an infertility problem of a married couple. The drugs could not licitly be used as part of a prohibited procedure, such as in vitro fertilization. Rather, they could only be used to help the spouses' conjugal act "reach its natural objectives." As *Donum Vitae* said, "If the technical means facilitates the conjugal act or helps it to reach its natural objectives, it can be morally acceptable. If, on the other hand, the procedure were to replace the conjugal act, it is morally illicit" [II, B, 6].
>
> The spouses must be fully aware of the risk for multiple ovulations from these drugs. If possible, the couple should learn whether some dosages have a greater risk of multiple ovula-

tions and avoid such a dosage, depending upon what it is. Multiple ovulations can result in multiple conceptions, which can lead to serious pregnancy complications. The couple must be prepared to care for more than one child in the event that there are multiple births due to the use of the drugs. The couple should also consider other morally acceptable procedures.

## Compassion for Childless Couples

We cannot leave this subject without demonstrating that the Church is not insensitive to the plight of couples who are unable to conceive a child. The Church is both mother and teacher (*Mater et Magistra*, as Pope John XXIII said), and is constantly concerned about her children, with their successes and joys as well as their failures and sufferings. Somehow in the plan of God couples who want children are unable to have them, while at the same time, and with a bitter irony, some who are able to conceive children abort them.

The Church encourages those in the fields of science and medicine to do all that is moral in their power to help childless couples. And *Donum Vitae* offers this counsel:

> The suffering of spouses who cannot have children or who are afraid of bringing a handicapped child into the world is a suffering that everyone must understand and properly evaluate. On the part of the spouses, the desire for a child is natural: it expresses the vocation to fatherhood and motherhood inscribed in conjugal love. This desire can be even stronger if the couple is affected by sterility which appears incurable. Nevertheless, marriage does not confer upon the spouses the right to have a child, but only the right to perform those natural acts which are per se ordered to procreation.
>
> A true and proper right to a child would be contrary to the child's dignity and nature. The child is not an object to which one has a right, nor can he be considered as an object of ownership: rather, a child is a gift, " the supreme gift" and the most gratuitous gift of marriage, and is a living testimony of the mutual giving of his parents. For this reason, the child has the right, as already mentioned, to be the fruit of the specific act of the conjugal love of his parents; and he also has the right to be respected as a person from the moment of his conception.

Nevertheless, whatever its cause or prognosis, sterility is certainly a difficult trial. The community of believers is called to shed light upon and support the suffering of those who are unable to fulfill their legitimate aspiration to motherhood and fatherhood. Spouses who find themselves in this sad situation are called to find in it an opportunity for sharing in a particular way in the Lord's Cross, the source of spiritual fruitfulness.

Sterile couples must not forget that "even when procreation is not possible, conjugal life does not for this reason lose its value. Physical sterility, in fact, can be for spouses the occasion for other important services to the life of the human person, for example, adoption, various forms of educational work, and assistance to other families and to poor or handicapped children."

Many researchers are engaged in the fight against sterility. While fully safeguarding the dignity of human procreation, some have achieved results which previously seemed unattainable. Scientists therefore are to be encouraged to continue their research with the aim of preventing the causes of sterility and of being able to remedy them so that sterile couples will be able to procreate in full respect for their own personal dignity and that of the child to be born (Part II, 8).

## Discussion Questions and Projects:

1. How has widespread acceptance of contraception affected society over the past 30 years?
2. Explain to a critic why the Catholic Church cannot change its opposition to artificial contraception.
3. How is Natural Family Planning different from artificial methods of contraception?
4. Show how Pope Paul's predictions in *Humanae Vitae* have come true.
5. Refute the current theory that Onan was struck dead because he violated the law requiring him to marry his dead brother's widow.
6. Explain the difference between a contraceptive and an abortifacient.
7. Draw up a convincing argument that abstinence from sex is not impossible.
8. What are the dangers of cloning?
9. What is in vitro fertilization and why is the Church opposed to it?
10. What is wrong with surrogate motherhood?
11. What are the conditions under which assisted artificial insemination could be moral?
12. Under what circumstances is it morally allowable to use amniocentesis?
13. Is it always a good idea to take fertility drugs?
14. What advice would you give to childless couples?

Chapter 8

# Principles Relating to the Taking of Life

God alone is the Lord of life from its beginning until its end; no one can under any circumstances claim for himself the right directly to destroy an innocent human life. —*Catechism of the Catholic Church*, n. 2258

One cannot own anything until he is already alive. Life is a prerequisite to ownership. Perhaps that is what Thomas Jefferson had in mind when, in the Declaration of Independence, he put the right to life ahead of liberty and the pursuit of happiness as inalienable rights that we get from God and that no government can take away. In fact, the primary purpose of government is to protect our God-given rights. Without the basic right to life, no other rights have any meaning.

No person owns his life. The owner of each human life is God. We find it hard to understand why some persons given life by God suffer from certain physical or mental defects. Our human intellects are unable to fathom why an infinitely wise and loving Creator would allow this to happen. But the fact that this presents a problem to our limited intellects does not bestow on us the authority to judge that God made a mistake or the power to remedy that "mistake" by ending the existence of a life that God, as part of his creative plan, chose to send into the world.

We must remember, then, that the same God who gave us our life also made us custodians or stewards of that life, as well as of the lives of our brothers and sisters in the Lord. We have the solemn duty of protecting and conserving our life and the lives of others until such time as the Almighty, and no one else, decides to take the gift of life away from us. In the words of *Donum Vitae*:

> The gift of life which God the Creator and Father has entrusted to man calls him to appreciate the inestimable value of what he has been given and to take responsibility for it: this fundamental principle must be placed at the center of one's reflection in order to clarify and solve the moral problems raised by artificial interventions on life as it originates and on the process of procreation (Introduction, 1).

## The Culture of Death

The increasing threats to human life in our time, particularly toward the weakest and most defenseless members of the human family — the unborn, the handicapped, the elderly — prompted Pope John Paul II to issue an encyclical on "The Gospel of Life" (*Evangelium Vitae*). He said that the encyclical was "meant to be a precise and vigorous reaffirmation of the value of human life and its inviolability, and at the same time a pressing appeal addressed to each and every person in the name of God: **Respect, protect, love, and serve life, every human life!** Only in this direction will you find justice, development, true freedom, peace, and happiness! (n. 5).

Summarizing the problem, the Holy Father said that "we are in fact faced by an objective 'conspiracy against life,' involving even international institutions engaged in encouraging and carrying out actual campaigns to make contraception, sterilization, and abortion widely available. Nor can it be denied that the mass media are often implicated in this conspiracy, by lending credit to that culture which presents recourse to contraception, sterilization, abortion, and even euthanasia as a mark of progress and a victory of freedom, while depicting as enemies of freedom and progress those positions which are unreservedly pro-life" (n. 17).

This situation, John Paul continued, "ought to make us fully aware that we are facing an enormous and dramatic clash between good and evil, death and life, the 'culture of death' and the 'culture of life.' We find ourselves not only 'faced with' but necessarily 'in the midst of' this conflict: We are all involved and we all share in it, with the inescapable responsibility of choosing to be unconditionally pro-life" (n. 28).

He said that "Moses' invitation rings out loud and clear: 'See, I have set before you this day life and good, death and evil .... I have set before you life and death, blessing and curse; therefore choose life, that you and your descendants may live' (Dt. 30:15, 19). This invitation is very appropriate for us who are called day by day to the duty of choosing between the 'culture of life' and the 'culture of death' " (*Ibid.*).

But we should not feel overwhelmed with powerlessness, the Holy Father said, reminding us that Jesus is "the way, and the truth, and the life" (John 14:6); that our Lord promised that "whoever lives and believes in me shall never die" (John 11:26); and that Christ came to earth "that they may have life, and have it abundantly" (John 10:10).

The Pope said that "through the words, the actions, and the very person of Jesus, man is given the possibility of 'knowing' the complete truth concerning the value of human life. From this 'source' he receives in particular the capacity to 'accomplish' this truth perfectly (cf. Jn. 3:21), that is, to accept and fulfill completely the responsibility of loving and serving, of defending and promoting human life" (*Evangelium Vitae*, n. 29).

## The Right to Life

Because our life comes from God — "it is his gift, his image and imprint, a sharing in his breath of life" (n. 39) — we cannot do with life whatever we wish, said Pope John Paul. The Lord made this clear in the commandment that says "You shall not kill." Thus we are to show reverence for the life of every person. No one, Pope John Paul declared in *Evangelium Vitae* (n. 47), "can arbitrarily choose whether to live or die; the absolute master of such a decision is the Creator alone, 'in whom we live and move and have our being' " [Acts 17:28].

It is clear, then, that one may never directly take the life of an innocent human being. The two key words in that statement are "directly" and "innocent." A discussion of such things as legitimate self-defense, a just war, and capital punishment do not fall under the scope of medical ethics (these issues are fully covered in chapter seven of *Catholicism and Life*, a companion volume in this series), so we will take up only such matters as abortion, euthanasia, physician-assisted suicide, and the Catholic philosophy of redemptive suffering.

The events of the past century have established beyond a doubt that when anyone is allowed to take an innocent human life directly for any reason, the door is opened to the most horrible crimes, and society is soon plagued with murder, injustice, misery, and chaos. No one is secure in the possession of life, and fear and suspicion become widespread. This is what happened in Nazi Germany when euthanasia was legalized and the government claimed the right to liquidate anyone considered useless to the state.

Recall, too, that it was not Hitler himself who created the German euthanasia program, but rather certain physicians. It was the professors of psychiatry from twelve major German universities who designed the first gas chamber, selected the patients, and watched them die. Mental patients were the first victims, then handicapped children, and finally children whose only "crime" was bed-wetting (cf. Frederic Wertham, M.D., *The German Euthanasia Program* and *A Sign for Cain*, and William Brennan, *The Abortion Holocaust*). Hitler then used these gas chambers to eliminate millions of Jews, Gypsies, and Catholics.

As the general public becomes more aware of the violations of God's dominion over life by certain members of the medical profession, there is a growing sense of unease and distrust that threatens the high esteem in which this once-great profession was held. How can a person respect a physician who murders unborn children? The word "abortionist" was once a term of opprobrium that no doctor would want to be called, but as the death toll from legal abortion in the United States continues at a rate of more than one million babies killed each year, the stigma lessens for those doctors who have become killers instead of curers.

The same lessening of revulsion on the part of many people is also true regarding doctors who take the lives of their elderly or sick patients under the euphemism of "mercy killing." But there is at the same time an increasing fear on the part of patients who have put themselves in the hands of physicians who may decide to kill any patient who is no longer leading a life that some segments of society would consider "useful." And pressure from family members and physicians has even pushed some people into requesting assistance in committing suicide.

These violations of our God-given right to life, which have moved from theory into daily practice in recent decades, are taking their toll on society. Life has become cheaper with the passing years, and we find ourselves facing a situation where concerted action is needed if we are to stop this erosion of respect for human life. For if an innocent life can be snuffed out at the beginning because the child is not planned, perfect, or privileged, so, too, innocent life can be terminated at the other end of the spectrum for social, financial, or other reasons. It is not a pleasant scenario to contemplate.

## Abortion

**Abortion is the expulsion of a non-viable fetus, or the deliberate killing of an unborn child in the womb.** The expulsion may be deliberate or accidental; it may be threatened, incomplete, or complete. Moral problems arise if the unborn child is alive. We can divide abortion into three major classifications: (1) spontaneous, (2) indirect, and (3) direct. Spontaneous abortions may be threatened or inevitable, complete or incomplete.

**Spontaneous abortion** — A spontaneous abortion is that which is caused by disease or accident. It is the unintentional expulsion of a baby and is sometimes called a miscarriage. When there is bleeding, the outcome of which is doubtful, the abortion is known as a threatened abortion. On the other hand, if it appears certain that the child will be expelled, the term "inevitable abortion" is used. If the baby has already been expelled but some afterbirth and membranes remain, the abortion is referred to as incomplete. This presents no moral problem, but there could be medical problems, such as infection, if all the remains are not removed.

If the spontaneous abortion is merely threatened, in most cases bed rest and appropriate medications are the treatments indicated. Termination by curretage (scraping the baby from the uterine wall with a sharp instrument), which is sometimes advised in this case, would be morally as well as obstetrically wrong. Packing or the use of a tampon would also be immoral under the circumstances.

If the spontaneous abortion seems to be inevitable, that is, the cervix is dilating of its own accord, and the patient is hemorrhaging and is in immediate danger of bleeding to death, surgical intervention is indicated. The operation is referred to as dilatation and curretage ("D and C").

Surgical intervention is licit if the placenta has become detached because then the baby has already expired from lack of oxygen. Before the placenta becomes detached, however, a D and C would constitute a direct attack on the life of the child and would be immoral.

By the time the mother is brought into the operating room, the baby has almost always been expelled. And in those rare cases in which it has not been expelled, it is morally certain that the baby is dead. Therefore, the doctor has a moral certitude that there is no living child present.

Swift death by exsanguination (severe hemorrhage) threatens the mother and, in order to save her life, the doctor proceeds on the basis of his moral certitude that the child is dead. Emptying the uterus is permissible when the physician is reasonably sure that the baby is already dead or already detached. In the case of an incomplete abortion, no moral problems exist since the unborn child has already been expelled.

**Indirect abortion** — An indirect abortion is the foreseen (as least with probability) but unintended loss of the baby following a medical procedure necessary to preserve the life or health of the mother. The baby is in no way directly attacked, and the loss of fetal life is a secondary and unintentional consequence. For example, the removal of an acutely infected appendix might be necessary to save the mother's life, but there is a great risk to the life of the child she is carrying.

Surgery at this time is permissible by reason of the principle of the twofold effect: the act is morally indifferent, it produces a good effect which does not follow from the evil effect, the motive is good, and the good effect at least equals the evil which may result. This situation is morally similar to tubal pregnancy or a cancerous uterus.

**Direct abortion** — A direct or induced abortion is the deliberate termination of pregnancy, the only immediate purpose of which is the destruction of the unborn baby. Therapeutic abortion is an abortion induced directly and deliberately for the purpose of saving the mother's life or health. Since this type of abortion is a direct attack on an innocent life, the principle of the twofold effect does not apply because any good which results from the abortion arises by the performance of an evil act. The health of one person is preserved by the direct murder of another person.

The Church's opposition to direct abortion goes all the way back to the *Didache*, a first-century collection of the teachings of the Apostles, which states: "You shall not procure abortion. You shall not destroy a newborn child." That opposition was later expressed by Athenagoras in the second century, Jerome in the fourth century, Augustine in the fifth century, Pope Stephen V in the ninth century, Aquinas in the 13th century, Pope Sixtus V in the 16th century, and by virtually every Pope in the 20th century, as well as by the Second Vatican Council and the *Catechism of the Catholic Church*.

Now some have claimed that the Church's teaching on abortion evolved over the centuries and that she did not always condemn abortion. That is false. There was a time in the Middle Ages when it was thought that the soul was not present in the unborn child until weeks after conception. So a distinction was made in the evaluation of the sin and the gravity of the penalty imposed for abortions performed in the first few weeks after conception and those performed after the soul was believed to be present. But at no time did those Catholic moralists holding this opinion ever deny that procured abortion was an objectively grave evil.

On October 29, 1951, Pope Pius XII said that "every human being, even a child in the uterus of its mother, has a right to life directly from God, and not from its parents or from any human society or authority. Therefore, there is no man, no human authority, no science; there is no medical, eugenic, social, economic, or moral 'indication' that can offer or produce a valid juridical title to a direct, deliberate disposal of an innocent human life."

## Modern Condemnations of Abortion

The Second Vatican Council (1962-1965) called abortion an "unspeakable crime" (*Pastoral Constitution on the Church in the Modern World*, n. 51), and the *Catechism of the Catholic Church* stated:

> Human life must be respected and protected absolutely from the moment of conception. From the first moment of his existence, a human being must be recognized as having the rights of a person — among which is the inviolable right of every innocent being to life (n. 2270).
>
> Since the first century the Church has affirmed the moral evil of every procured abortion. This teaching has not changed and remains unchangeable. Direct abortion, that is to say, abortion willed either as an end or a means, is gravely contrary to the moral law (n. 2271).

There are some today who say that since the Church has not spoken out infallibly on this issue, Catholics can follow their conscience and remain Catholics in good standing while taking a pro-abortion stance. But Catholics are obliged to assent to the teachings of the Holy Father even when he does not speak infallibly (cf. Vatican II, *Dogmatic Constitution on the Church*, n. 25), particu-

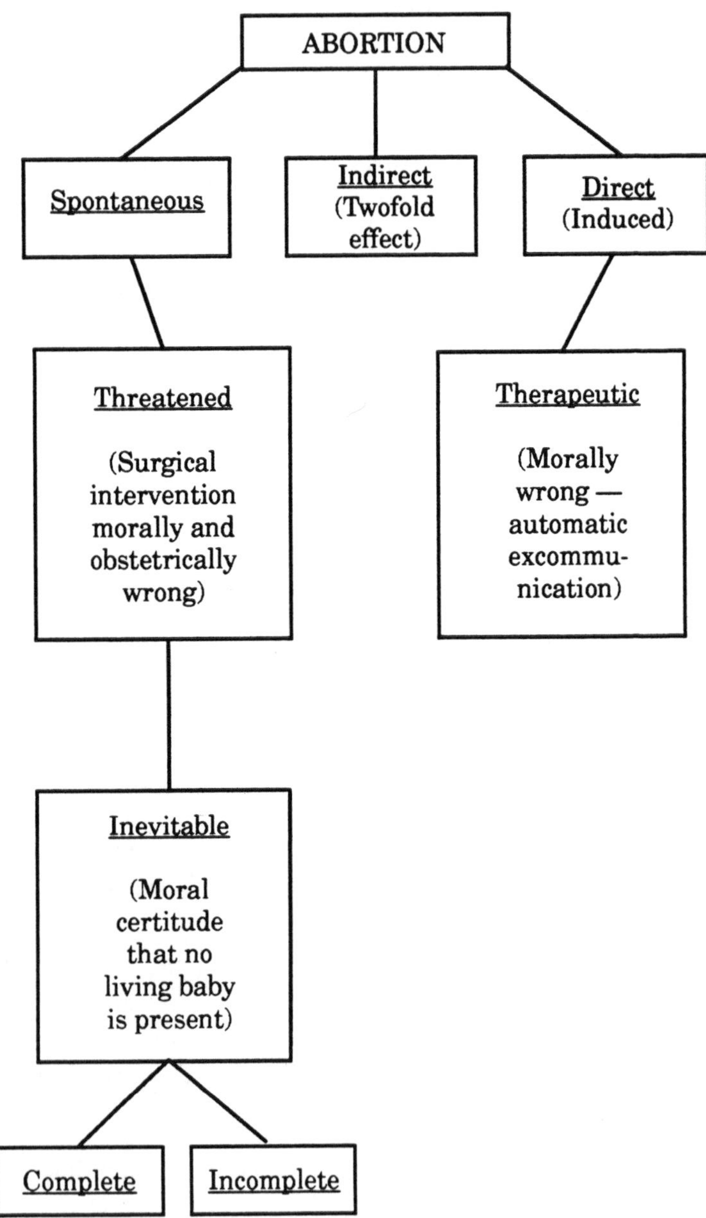


*The Morality of Abortion*

larly on an issue like abortion, which the Church has so vigorously condemned for 20 centuries.

Furthermore, in 1995, Pope John Paul II came about as close to an infallible statement as is possible when he declared:

> Therefore, by the authority which Christ conferred upon Peter and his successors, in communion with the bishops — who on various occasions have condemned abortion and who ... have shown unanimous agreement concerning this doctrine — **I declare that direct abortion, that is, abortion willed as an end or as a means, always constitutes a grave moral disorder, since it is the deliberate killing of an innocent human being**. This doctrine is based upon the natural law and upon the written word of God, is transmitted by the Church's tradition and taught by the ordinary and universal Magisterium (*Evangelium Vitae*, n. 62).

## The Penalty of Excommunication

So strongly does the Church feel about abortion, in fact, that she imposes the penalty of excommunication (canon 1398 of the Code of Canon Law) on all those involved in the deliberate and successful effort to bring about a completed abortion. This affects, said Pope John Paul in *Evangelium Vitae*, "all those who commit this crime with knowledge of the penalty attached and thus includes those accomplices without whose help the crime would not have been committed. By this reiterated sanction, the Church makes clear that abortion is a most serious and dangerous crime, thereby encouraging those who commit it to seek without delay the path of conversion" (n. 62).

According to canons 1323 and 1324 of the Code of Canon Law, excommunication would not be automatically incurred if a person was truly ignorant of the penalty attached to procuring an abortion, was under the age of 16, thought that the law applied only to the person having the abortion and not to her accomplices, acted out of serious fear about parental or societal reaction to the pregnancy, or erroneously believed that the abortion was necessary and permissible to preserve the mother's life.

## No Good Reason for Abortion

Those who argue for keeping abortion legal often talk about safeguarding the life or health of the mother, or say that this option should be available in cases of pregnancy resulting from rape or incest. But with the advances in medical science, there are virtually no medical indications for abortion. Doctors are able to bring to term pregnancies faced with a variety of complications. And even if abortion were permitted in cases of rape or incest, it would involve at most one or two percent of the 1.5 million abortions reported in the United States each year.

By the way, the innocent victim of a criminal rape is allowed to destroy the sperm before conception takes place on the grounds that one may resist unjust aggression. A victim of rape should get to a hospital as quickly as possible so that the sperm can be removed from the vagina since conception does not take place there. If any means is used to remove the sperm from the uterus or from the fallopian tubes, it must be employed before there is any probability that conception has taken place. Abortion is not morally permissible even when the pregnancy results from rape.

So the primary reason why women seek abortions is that they don't want a child at this particular time. Some cite problems involving education, career, finances, etc. But whatever the problem, the solution must be to get rid of the problem, not the baby. If a mother-to-be does not want to raise a child at this time, she can put the baby up for adoption. There are literally tens of thousands of couples who are desperately trying to adopt; some of them are even spending large sums of money and traveling to foreign countries seeking children. How ironic it is that we are killing healthy babies who could fulfill the longing of childless couples!

We cannot ignore the fact that for some people, abortion is a backup for failed contraception. Here is how one proponent of abortion, Germaine Greer, puts it:

> Abortion is an extension of contraceptive technology, and the most promising extension of it at that. Abortion is not a stopgap between here and some future perfect contraceptive; it can very well be the chosen method of birth control for more and more women (Germaine Greer, *Sex and Destiny*, p. 231).

## Partial-Birth Abortion

All forms of abortion are gruesome, but the most horrific is the one known as "partial-birth abortion." This involves the feet-first delivery of an infant up to the level of his head. The base of the baby's skull is then punctured with a sharp instrument, the brain contents are sucked out, collapsing the skull, and a dead child is delivered. This procedure is mostly performed in the fifth and sixth months, but has been performed up to the ninth month of pregnancy, allegedly for health reasons, but physicians have testified that there is no need for partial-birth abortion even in cases involving trisomy (extra chromosomal material), hydrocephaly (water on the brain), and polyhydramnios (too much amniotic fluid).

In testimony before a joint hearing of the U.S. House and Senate Judiciary Committees on March 11, 1997, Dr. Curtis Cook, a specialist in high-risk obstetrics, said that "I have personally cared for many cases of all of these disorders, and have never required any technique like partial-birth abortion in order to accomplish delivery." He said that "the only possible 'advantage' of partial-birth abortion, if you can call it that, is that it guarantees a dead baby at time of delivery" (*National Right to Life News*, April 8, 1997, p. 8).

Dr. Cook also testified that these techniques, which are performed thousands of times a year, "place the woman at greater risk for both immediate (bleeding) and delayed (infection) complications. In fact, there may also be longer repercussions of cervical manipulation leading to an inherent weakness of the cervix and the inability to carry pregnancies to term. We have already seen women who have had trouble maintaining pregnancies after undergoing a partial-birth abortion" (*Ibid.*).

One of the best-kept secrets of the abortion industry is the serious physical and mental complications that women have experienced following so-called "safe, legal abortions." For documentation of this, see David C. Reardon's book *Aborted Women: Silent No More*. See also the book *Blood Money: Getting Rich off a Woman's Right to Choose* by Carol Everett, who ran two abortion facilities and who describes the lies, the callousness, and the chaos that characterize these places where killing babies is the reason for their existence.

The devil is surely the patron of these abortion chambers where lying and murdering are the order of the day, for it was Christ himself who called Satan the "father of lies" and a "murderer from the beginning" (cf. John 8:44).

## Compassion for Victims of Abortion

The unborn child is the first victim of abortion, and the mother is the second victim. While we condemn the sin of abortion, we do not condemn the sinner and particularly not those who have been pressured into abortion and exploited by others. There are many church and community groups which offer love, compassion, and support to those faced with unwanted pregnancies, and healing to those who have had abortions. Those wishing to reach out to women in these situations ought to become involved with crisis pregnancy centers and groups like Birthright and Project Rachel.

One person who has extended a loving hand to women who have had abortions is Pope John Paul, who offered these women a special word of hope and encouragement in his encyclical *Evangelium Vitae*:

> The Church is aware of the many factors which may have influenced your decision, and she does not doubt that in many cases it was a painful and even shattering decision. The wound in your heart may not yet have healed. Certainly what happened was and remains terribly wrong. But do not give in to discouragement and do not lose hope. Try rather to understand what happened and face it honestly. If you have not already done so, give yourselves over with humility and trust to repentance. The Father of mercies is ready to give you his forgiveness and his peace in the sacrament of Reconciliation.
>
> You will come to understand that nothing is definitively lost, and you will also be able to ask forgiveness from your child, who is now living in the Lord. With the friendly and expert help and advice of other people and as a result of your own painful experience, you can be among the most eloquent defenders of everyone's right to life. Through your commitment to life, whether by accepting the birth of other children or by welcoming and caring for those most in need of someone to be close to them, you will become promoters of a new way of looking at human life (n. 99).

## Baptism of the Fetus

We should make a few comments relative to the baptism of a fetus. This tiny unborn child is endowed with an immortal soul and is destined for union with God for all eternity. Therefore, every child should be baptized if the opportunity presents itself. This holds true regardless of the immaturity of the baby or of the circumstances which have brought about its separation from the body of the mother.

Anyone, even a non-Christian, can baptize in an emergency. All one has to do is to pour the water over the baby's head and pronounce the words, "I baptize you in the name of the Father, and of the Son, and of the Holy Spirit." If the person intends what the Church intends and uses water and the Trinitarian formula, then the child is validly baptized.

## Induction of Labor

**Induction of labor is the act of initiating delivery of a viable baby prior to spontaneous delivery**. There are two kinds: an indicated induction, which is initiated to cure or alleviate a pathologic condition, and an elective induction, which is initiated in the absence of any medical indication. In making a decision about induction, one must determine the viability of the child, i.e., the child's ability to survive outside the mother's womb. This is a matter that can change with advances in medical technology and the study of the unborn child (fetology), and doctors are currently able to save babies that are born between 20 and 24 weeks of pregnancy.

Determination of viability rests upon the prudent judgment of a competent obstetrician after due consideration of medical principles in relation to particular circumstances. It is possible, of course, that the subsequent death of the baby may seem to show that the doctor's opinion was wrong. There is no need for a troubled conscience, however, as long as the doctor made a sincere and cautious judgment. But the direct initiation of delivery prior to viability is direct abortion and is a serious violation of the moral law.

## The Morality of Indicated Induction

When the induction of a viable baby is medically indicated (required for a very good medical reason), it is morally right. This conclusion is based on the principle of the double effect. For example, the good effect of an indicated induction is the cure or alleviation of a disease; the bad effect is the danger to the premature child. The good effect, as we noted in chapter four, must follow from the action itself, and not from the bad effect. There being no less dangerous procedure available, and the pathologic condition being of sufficient gravity to give a proper proportion between the good and bad effects, it is moral to induce labor.

Obviously, induction should be delayed as long as safety allows, but when the induction of a viable child is medically indicated, it is morally right.

## The Morality of Elective Induction

For the purposes of this discussion, we may divide elective induction into three kinds: harmful, risky, and harmless. We do not presume to state whether there is truly such a thing as a harmless induction; that is a medical matter. We simply state the moral principle that would apply if there is a completely harmless elective induction. Determination of the harmlessness of an elective procedure rests upon the conscience of the physician. The presumption is in favor of nature; the burden of proof as to the harmlessness of intervention into a natural healthy process rests with the doctor.

Harmful elective induction, i.e., a procedure that will certainly harm mother or child, is not morally allowable. The principle of the twofold effect will not apply in this case because there is not a proper proportion between human life or health and such things as convenience, money, or sentiment (e.g., having the baby on the same day her mother had her). A certainly harmful elective induction is bad morals and bad medicine.

A risky elective induction is one where it is not morally right to risk human life or health without a proportionately grave reason. In the absence of any pathologic condition, it is difficult to imagine a sufficiently grave reason that would allow the obstetrician to chance an induction that might harm mother or child. Such things as convenience, financial considerations, social obligations, or sentimental motives should not be weighed in the balance against a person's physical or mental well-being.

A harmless elective induction, one in which the obstetrician is morally certain that induction will involve no more risk than normal delivery, can be considered merely an acceleration of the natural process rather than an interference with it. This sort of elective induction would be morally allowable for a sufficient reason, even if the reason is a non-medical one. It is not to be preferred, however, because medicine is at its best when it leaves to nature a process that is healthy, normal, and natural. All things being equal, it seems problematic to argue that intervention in a healthy natural process is as good as non-intervention.

In judging a sufficient or proportionate reason relative to these cases, the earlier the induction is initiated, the more serious the reason must be. It does not seem morally right to anticipate delivery by more than a few days. Elective induction is morally allowable only if there is a moral certitude that it involves no more risk than spontaneous delivery.

To sum up: (1) The direct initiation of delivery prior to viability is direct abortion and a serious violation of the natural law. (2) When induction is medically indicated, it is morally right. (3) Elective induction is morally justifiable only if there is moral certitude that it involves no more risk than normal delivery.

We conclude this section with the clear teaching of the Second Vatican Council:

> From the moment of its conception life must be guarded with the greatest care, while abortion and infanticide are unspeakable crimes (*Pastoral Constitution on the Church in the Modern World*, n. 51).

## Euthanasia

While often euphemistically called "mercy killing," the Church defines euthanasia as **"an action or omission which of itself and by intention causes death, with the purpose of eliminating all suffering"** (*Evangelium Vitae*, n. 65). This is not the same thing as forgoing medical treatments which no longer correspond to the real situation of the patient either because they are disproportionate to any expected results or because they impose an excessive burden on the patient and his family, said Pope John Paul. For the Church has always taught that "one can in conscience 'refuse forms of treatment that would only secure a precarious and burdensome prolongation of life, so long as the normal care due to a sick person in similar cases is not interrupted' " (*Ibid.*).

There is always a moral obligation to take care of oneself and to allow others to care for us, the Holy Father continued, "but this duty must take account of concrete circumstances. It needs to be determined whether the means of treatment available are objectively proportionate to the prospects for improvement. To forgo extraordinary or disproportionate means is not the equivalent of suicide or euthanasia; it rather expresses acceptance of the human condition in the face of death" (*Ibid.*).

Proponents of euthanasia, "death with dignity," and physician-assisted suicide present their case through emotional arguments that play on people's fears of suffering through unbearable pain, loss of independence and personal dignity, and expensive but futile treatments that only drag out the dying process and put the patient through a living hell. However, when their arguments are reduced to their true substance, they come down to the following:

(1) You would kill an animal in pain. Why not do as much for a human being?

(2) Why condemn anyone to spend their final days in misery?

(3) Mercy killing or physician-assisted suicide would be painless.

(4) Euthanasia or physician-assisted suicide would relieve the family of a financial burden and an emotional strain.

(5) Euthanasia or physician-assisted suicide would also relieve society of a financial burden.

## Reasons Why Euthanasia Is Wrong

Despite the emotional arguments, however, there are many reasons why the legalized killing of patients with lethal drugs or by other means would be morally and socially wrong:

(1) Legalized euthanasia or physician-assisted suicide entail the direct killing of persons.

(2) Killing is incompatible with caring, and it is the elderly, the disabled, and the poor who will be put at risk.

(3) The purpose of the medical profession is to preserve life, not destroy it. Doctors who cure and heal should not be agents of death. Legalized euthanasia would make a doctor a person to be feared rather than a person to be trusted.

(4) The legal permission to die can easily become the duty to die. Terminally ill patients will feel pressured to die to spare their families or their communities an emotional and financial burden.

(5) Unscrupulous persons will try to arrange for the death of an enemy or a wealthy relative.

(6) Doctors in the Netherlands, where physician-assisted suicide has been legal for years, annually kill hundreds of patients *who did not request death.*

(7) Legalized euthanasia would lessen the incentive for medical research to cure some terminal illnesses or to lessen the suffering of those afflicted with them.

(8) Some patients surprise doctors by coming out of comas or by recovering from terminal illnesses; legalized euthanasia would kill them first.

(9) Patients in most states already have the legal right to refuse any treatment they don't want. Dying is not "undignified"; it is part of being human.

(10) With competent medical care, no one needs to die in unrelenting pain. Doctors should kill the pain, not the patient.

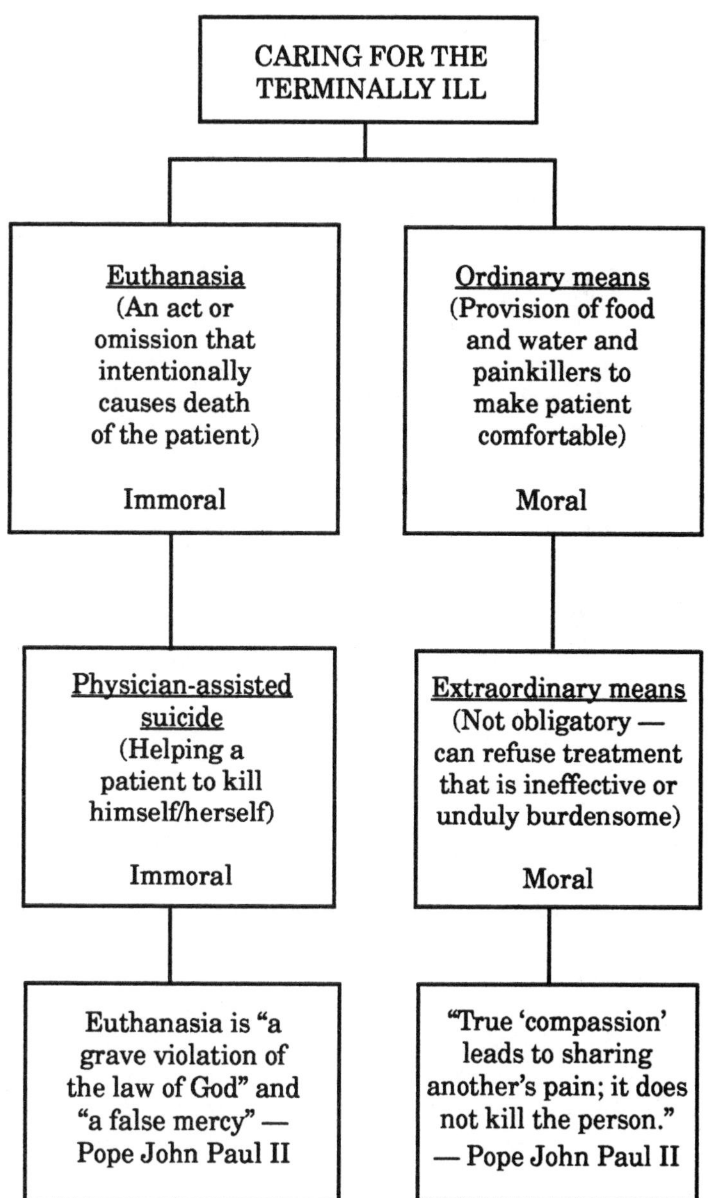


*The Morality of Euthanasia*

It is time to call euthanasia and physician-assisted suicide by their correct name, and that name is murder. Even the president of the pro-euthanasia Nebraska Hemlock Society, a man named Carl Schmitthausler, was honest enough to say: "When you strip away all the euphemisms, we're talking about doctors killing patients" *(Lincoln Journal Star*, December 30, 1995).

## Assisted Suicide Also Wrong

Helping a person to kill himself or herself is just as wrong as murder. In the words of Pope John Paul:

> To concur with the intention of another person to commit suicide and to help in carrying it out through so-called "assisted suicide" means to cooperate in and at times to be the actual perpetrator of an injustice which can never be excused. In a remarkably relevant passage, St. Augustine writes that "it is never licit to kill another: even if he should wish it, indeed if he request it, because, hanging between life and death, he begs for help in freeing the soul struggling against the bonds of the body and longing to be released; nor is it licit even when a sick person is no longer able to live" (*Evangelium Vitae*, n. 66).

Euthanasia is "a false mercy and indeed a disturbing 'perversion' of mercy," said Pope John Paul. "True 'compassion' leads to sharing another's pain; it does not kill the person whose suffering we cannot bear. Moreover, the act of euthanasia appears all the more perverse if it is carried out by those, like relatives, who are supposed to treat a family member with patience and love, or by those, such as doctors, who by virtue of their specific profession are supposed to care for the sick person even in the most painful terminal stages" (n. 66).

As impractical and harmful as the legalization of euthanasia would be, the basic reason for rejecting it is a moral one. Euthanasia is a bold and outrageous infringement upon the sovereign rights of Almighty God. God alone, as our Creator, has dominion over life. Our life is to end when God so wills and not before. When a person dares to terminate a human life, he is guilty of serious immorality. Such conduct cannot be made right by the passage of any sort of legisation by any authority on earth.

Taking all of this into account and in communion with all the bishops of the world, Pope John Paul made this unequivocal declaration in *Evangelium Vitae* (n. 65):

> I confirm that euthanasia is a grave violation of the law of God, since it is the deliberate and morally unacceptable killing of a human person. This doctrine is based upon the natural law and upon the written word of God, is transmitted by the Church's tradition and taught by the ordinary and universal Magisterium. Depending on the circumstances, this practice involves the malice proper to suicide or murder.

## Narcotics to the Dying

It is a common practice to give narcotics to a person when death is approaching. This is morally justified, provided that certain conditions are fulfilled. These conditions include (1) the opportunity for receiving the sacraments has been given (in the case of a Catholic); (2) there is severe physical pain to be relieved; and (3) the dose is not intentionally lethal. We say "intentionally" because a patient could build up an increasing tolerance to a higher dosage of a narcotic, say, morphine, and the level of dosage required to alleviate the pain could be *unintentionally* lethal. This would be permissible under the principle of the double effect.

Addressing this subject before a Symposium on Anesthesiology on February 24, 1957, Pope Pius XII asked three questions:

(1) Is there a universal moral obligation to refuse analgesia and to accept physical pain in the spirit of faith?

(2) Is it in accord with the spirit of the Gospel to bring about by means of drugs the loss of consciousness and of the use of a person's faculties?

(3) Is it lawful for the dying or those in danger of death to make use of drugs, even if lessening of pain is probably accompanied by a shortening of life?

Essentially the Holy Father answered "no" to the first question and "yes" to the second and third. Here are a few of his important observations in that address:

> The patient desirous of avoiding or lessening pain can in good conscience make use of the means discovered by science which in themselves are not immoral. The Christian's duty of renunciation and of interior purification is not an obstacle to the use of anesthetics. Narcosis involving a lessening or a suppression of consciousness is permitted by natural morality and is in keeping with the spirit of the Gospel.

> If the dying person has fulfilled all his duties and received the last sacraments, if medical reasons clearly suggest the use of drugs, if in determining the dose the permitted amount is not exceeded, if the intensity and duration of the treatment is carefully calculated and the patient consents to it, then there is no objection. The use of drugs is morally permissible.

Referring back some 38 years later to the teaching of Pius XII, Pope John Paul said that "while praise may be due to the person who voluntarily accepts suffering by forgoing treatment with pain-killers in order to remain fully lucid and, if a believer, to share consciously in the Lord's Passion, such 'heroic' behavior cannot be considered the duty of everyone." He said that in resorting to narcotics, "death is not willed or sought, even though for reasonable motives one runs the risk of it: There is simply a desire to ease pain effectively by using the analgesics which medicine provides."

All the same, the Holy Father continued, " 'it is not right to deprive a dying person of consciousness without a serious reason.' As they approach death people ought to be able to satisfy their moral and family duties, and above all they ought to be able to prepare in a fully conscious way for the definitive meeting with God" (*Evangelium Vitae*, n. 65).

To deprive a patient of consciousness before he has had the opportunity to confess his sins and to receive the sacraments devoutly is, at best, to deprive him of much spiritual merit and, at worst, to take away his last chance for salvation. It is not morally right to administer narcotics to the dying to relieve mental stress. If there is no severe physical pain, the patient should be left conscious for as long as his consciousness is not taken away by God.

When an extremely weak patient has excruciating pain, narcotics may be administered, even though there is a danger of shortening his life. This is permissible by application of the principle of the twofold effect because the reason for the administration of such medication is to relieve pain and not to cause death. Deliberately giving a lethal dose of narcotics to a patient, as noted above, is murder.

During his pontificate, Pope John Paul II wrote extensively on the plight of the seriously sick, those with disabilities, and the suffering. What he said in two talks, on March 28 and May 28, 1982, puts into perspective the matters discussed in this chapter:

> The Lord does not ask us to close our eyes to infirmity. It is very real, and we must have a clear awareness of it. He asks

us to look more deeply, to believe that in these suffering bodies there throbs not only human life with all its dignity and rights, but also, by virtue of Baptism, divine life itself, the marvelous life of children of God. If to the external eyes of men you appear weak and infirm, before God you are great and brilliant in your being.

I support with all my heart those who recognize and defend the law of God which governs human life. We must never forget that every person, from the moment of conception to the last breath, is a unique child of God and has the right to life. This right should be defended by the attentive care of the medical and nursing professions and by the protection of the law. Every human life is willed by our heavenly Father and is a part of his loving plan.

## Advance Medical Directives for Health Care

In recent years there has been considerable discussion and at times recommendations concerning a person's desires at the time of serious and especially potentially terminal illness. Some feel that a simple statement of the patient's wishes would solve the problem, but this is not the case because there are practical, legal, and, not to be forgotten, moral implications.

The main thrust of our comments will focus on the moral dimension, with some reference to other considerations. As background for understanding and implementing this material, the reader should take into account the moral norms discussed in previous pages.

The most common advance medical directives recognized today are the living will and the durable power of attorney or health care proxy. We will take a close look at each of these options in light of Catholic teaching on the prolongation or termination of life. But before doing so, let us review Catholic teaching:

(1) No one owns his own life. God gave us our life and he owns it; we are only the stewards or guardians of that life and we have no right to "play God" and decide who shall live and who shall die.

(2) Euthanasia is an action or an omission which of itself or by intention causes death. It is an attack on human life which no one has the right to make or to request for himself or for another person. Although individual guilt may be mitigated because of suffering or emotional factors which cloud the conscience, this does

not change the objective evil of the act. An apparent plea for death may really be a plea for help and love.

(3) Suffering is a fact of human existence and has special significance for the Christian as an opportunity to share in Christ's redemptive suffering. Nevertheless, there is nothing wrong with trying to relieve one's suffering, provided it does not violate moral or religious norms. It is permissible in the case of terminal illness to use painkillers which carry the risk of shortening life as long as the intent is to relieve pain rather than cause death.

(4) Everyone has the duty to care for his or her own health and to seek necessary medical care from others, but this does not mean that all possible remedies must be used. One is not obliged to use extraordinary means in most cases.

**Living will** — A living will is a legal document that recognizes the right of a competent adult to give written instructions to physicians, hospitals, and other medical care providers regarding the use or withdrawal of life-sustaining procedures or treatments. It is a way of making life-and-death decisions before the actual need arises. Since living wills originated with, and have been vigorously promoted by, the pro-euthanasia movement, there is reason to be skeptical about them. Other reasons for concern are these:

(1) It is difficult to give informed consent in a general fashion for a medical situation that may occur some time in the future.

(2) The language of such documents is often vague and ambiguous. Phrases such as "extraordinary means," "terminally ill," "heroic measures," "reasonable expectation," or "no hope of recovery" are open to varying interpretations. The meaning of these terms can change with time and with individual patients.

(3) A person who signed a living will ten years ago could change his mind when the anticipated medical crisis arrives and opt for treatments he once spurned. But can he change his mind, or is the document he signed a decade earlier legally binding on the doctor?

(4) There is also the question of whether it is wise to let life-and-death decisions be made on the basis of what was written on a piece of paper years before.

**Durable power of attorney/health care proxy** — This document also spells out a person's wishes regarding life-sustaining procedures, but instead of being governed by a piece of paper, the person designates a trustworthy family member or friend, one with sound moral values, to act as his agent or proxy if the time should come when he is not competent to make medical decisions himself. The proxy would normally step into the picture after two physicians had declared the patient to be incompetent. The patient, of course, would retain decision-making power over his or her treatment until declared incompetent.

While these documents do not have the problems of living wills — they are based on actual situations, not hypothetical ones — nevertheless there are concerns about the person chosen to act as proxy, such as whether he might lose contact with the one who gave him the responsibility, or whether he might be unavailable when the medical decision has to be made, or whether he might make decisions contrary to the wishes of the patient.

Legally and morally speaking, the proxy is bound to carry out the patient's wishes — and the designator ought to have made quite clear to his agent what those wishes were both before and after he enlisted his services. One way of making sure the patient's desires are carried out would be to designate an alternate in case the first agent is not available. Another way would be to put copies of the document in the hands of doctors, family members, and friends who would insure that the directives are followed.

Another consideration is the diverse norms and limitations in effect in different states and in different medical institutions. Some places have policies against tube feeding and hydration and a surrogate would have to prove specific knowledge of the patient's wishes in order to supplant those policies. It is easy to see why anyone contemplating an advance medical directive ought to consult legal and moral authorities first. (See the sample health care proxy at the end of this chapter.)

## Conditions Necessitating Advance Directives

When deciding whether to invoke a durable power of attorney or health care proxy, the following situations would necessitate the use of an advance medical directive:

(1) When the treatment is experimental, likely to be ineffective or futile in prolonging life, or likely merely to prolong an imminent dying process.

(2) When the patient is permanently unconscious. A diagnosis of permanent unconsciousness must be made in writing by the attending physician and confirmed in writing by a second qualified doctor. Permanent unconsciousness includes, but is not limited to, a persistent vegetative state and irreversible coma.

(3) When the patient is in a terminal condition. A diagnosis of terminal condition must be made in writing by the attending physician and confirmed in writing by a second qualified doctor. A life expectancy of six months or less, with or without the provision of life-sustaining treatment, might reasonably be considered as terminal. However, a specific life expectancy is not required for a diagnosis of terminal condition.

(4) When a patient has a serious and irreversible illness or condition and (a) the likely risks and burdens of the treatment to be withheld or withdrawn may reasonably be judged to outweigh the likely benefits of the treatment to the patient, or (b) imposing the treatment on an unwilling patient in this condition would be inhumane. In these cases, the attending physician may seek consultation with a local reviewing body within the facility (such as an ethics committee) or a public agency prior to implementing the decision. However, while consultation with an ethics committee may be advisable, it is not necessarily required.

## The Christian Affirmation of Life

The Catholic Health Association has drawn up a document by which a person can indicate the treatment he would desire at the time of terminal illness. It is not intended to be a strictly legal document, but rather one of moral persuasion. However, it may have legal effects in some places, so the advice of an attorney is encouraged. Here is the text of the document:

**Christian Affirmation of Life**

To my family, friends, physician, lawyer, and clergyman:

I believe that each individual person is created by God our Father in love and that God retains a loving relationship to each person throughout human life and eternity.

I believe that Jesus Christ lived, suffered, and died for me and that his suffering, death, and resurrection prefigure and make possible the death-resurrection process which I now anticipate.

I believe that each person's worth and dignity derives from the relationship of love in Christ that God has for each individual person and not from one's usefulness or effectiveness in society.

I believe that God our Father has entrusted to me a shared dominion with him over my earthly existence so that I am bound to use ordinary means to preserve my life, but I am free to refuse extraordinary means to prolong my life.

I believe that through death life is not taken away but merely changed and, though I may experience fear, suffering, and sorrow, by the grace of the Holy Spirit I hope to accept death as a free human act which enables me to surrender this life and to be united with God for eternity.

Because of my belief:

I request that I be informed as death approaches. If I can no longer take part in decisions concerning my own future and if there is no reasonable expectation of my recovery from physical and mental disability, I request that no extraordinary means be used to prolong my life.

I request, though I wish to join my suffering to the suffering of Jesus so I may be united fully with him in the act of death-resurrection, that my pain, if unbearable, be alleviated. However, no means should be used with the intention of shortening my life.

I request, because I am a sinner and in need of reconciliation and because my faith, hope, and love may not overcome all fear and doubt, that my family, friends, and the whole Christian community join me in prayer and mortification as I prepare for the great personal act of dying.

Finally, I request that after my death, my family, my friends, and the whole Christian community pray for me and rejoice with me because of the mercy and love of the Trinity, with whom I hope to be united for all eternity.

Signed ______________________________ Date _____________

(Used with permission of the Catholic Health Association of the United States, St. Louis, Missouri)

## Some Final Thoughts

Most people at some time are faced with an unfortunate circumstance that befalls a loved one, or with a difficult decision involving oneself or someone close. Whatever the situation may be, never isolate it from the deep conviction that God is all-knowing, all-caring, and all-merciful.

You may be faced with a most difficult decision, indeed one that is heart-rending, for a person who is incapable of making the decision himself or herself. Recall that Holy Scripture reflects the basic truth that "there is a time to be born, and a time to die" (Ecclesiastes 3:2). This life is a preparation for an eternal life of peace and joy, a life of which St. Paul said: "Eye has not seen, ear has not heard, nor has it so much as dawned on man what God has prepared for those who love him" (1 Corinthians 2:9).

If difficult decisions must be made, do not make them alone. Talk to family and close friends, consult the clergy and medical personnel. And once a decision is carefully and conscientiously made, never have regrets or guilt feelings afterwards.

One thing that can be a consolation in the case of a sudden and unexpected death or when a decision is made to withdraw someone from life-support systems is to consider donating one's organs. The knowledge that the deceased person's death was the means of preserving another person's life or physical well-being is a great source of comfort.

What if the person is incompetent and with an imminent life-threatening prognosis? What if one has suffered a completely disabling stroke with heart and kidney failure? After sincere thought, competent advice, and evaluation of moral and ethical norms, you may in good conscience make a decision to rule out aggressive extraordinary technology. It is both ethical and moral to allow, but not will, the death of a terminally ill person without utilizing every possible medical procedure.

Sincere people are deeply conscious that life is precious, and it is often a traumatic and deeply emotional experience to render a life-and-death decision. Seek support from family, friends, medical personnel, and a clergyman who is experienced in dealing with such situations and who can understand what you are going through. Seek strength through prayer to the One who said, "Come to me all you who are weary and find life burdensome, and I will refresh you" (Matthew 11:28). And bring to your consciousness the feeling that in death, as well as in life, your only motivation has been and is love.

## Sample Health Care Proxy

### PREAMBLE

Because of my Catholic belief in the dignity of the human person and my eternal destiny in God, I ask that if I become terminally ill I be fully informed of the fact so that I can prepare myself emotionally and spiritually to die.

Life is a gift of a loving God. We see life as a sacred trust over which we can claim stewardship, but not ownership. Therefore, I believe that euthanasia and suicide constitute an unwarranted destruction of human life and are not morally permissible.

I understand that as a competent adult I have the right to make decisions about my health care. I understand, as a Catholic, that I may never choose to cause my death as an end or a means. There may come a time when I am unable, due to physical or mental incapacity, to express my own health care decisions. In these circumstances, those caring for me will need direction concerning my care and will turn to someone who knows my values and health care wishes. I direct that those responsible for my care seek to make health care decisions in accordance with what they know of my stated wishes. In order to provide the guidance and authority needed to implement my decisions:

If I become unable to make these decisions and have no reasonable expectation of recovery, then I request that no ethically extraordinary treatment be used to prolong my life, but that my pain be alleviated if it becomes unbearable, even if this results in shortening my life. ("Ethically extraordinary treatment" is treatment that does not offer a reasonable hope of benefit to me or that cannot be accomplished without excessive expense, pain, or other grave burden.) However, no treatment should be used with the intention of shortening my life.

I hereby declare and make known my instructions and wishes for my future health care. This advance directive for health care shall take effect in the event that I become unable to express my health care decisions, as determined by the physician who has primary responsibility for my care, and any necessary confirming determinations. I direct that this document become part of my permanent medical records.

I request that my family, my friends, and the Christian community join me in prayer as I prepare for death. I request that after my death others continue to pray for me so that I will, with God's grace, enjoy eternal life.

A. DESIGNATION OF A HEALTH CARE REPRESENTATIVE

I hereby designate: Name ____________________

Address ____________________

City/State ____________________

Telephone ____________________

as my health care representative to implement my health care decisions. I direct my representative to implement my health care decisions as stated in this document, or as otherwise known to him or her. In the event my wishes are not clear, or a situation arises I did not anticipate, my health care representative is authorized to make decisions based upon what he or she knows of my wishes. I have discussed the terms of this designation with my health care representative and he or she has willingly agreed to accept the responsibility for acting on my behalf.

B. ALTERNATE REPRESENTATIVE

If the person I have designated above is unable, unwilling, or unavailable to act as my health care representative, I hereby designate the following person(s) to act as my health care representative, in order of priority stated:

| 1. Name ____________________ | 2. Name ____________________ |
|---|---|
| Address ____________________ | Address ____________________ |
| City/State ____________________ | City/State ____________________ |
| Telephone ____________________ | Telephone ____________________ |

I have discussed the terms of this designation with my alternate health care representative(s) and he or she has willingly agreed to accept the responsibility for acting on my behalf.

C. INSTRUCTIONS

To inform those responsible for my care of my specific wishes, I direct that the following health care decisions be implemented:

1. A circumstance may arise when my attending physician and at least one additional physician who has personally examined me determine that the irreversible process of dying has begun and death is imminent. In that circumstance, I direct that measures which would serve only to prolong artificially my dying not be initiated and, if they have, they be discontinued. I also direct that I be given all medically appropriate care necessary to relieve pain and to make me comfortable.

2. A circumstance may arise when I have been diagnosed as being permanently comatose or being in a persistent vegetative state by my attending physician and at least one additional physician with appropriate expertise who has personally examined me. In that circumstance, I direct that extraordinary medical measures, as understood in the moral tradition of the Catholic Church, shall not be used. I direct that artificially provided food and water be continued unless or until the benefits of artificially provided food and water are clearly outweighed by a definite danger or burden to me, or are totally useless to me.

3. Extraordinary means of preserving life are characterized as all medicines, treatments, and operations which cannot be obtained without excessive expense, pain, or other inconvenience, or which, if used, would not offer a reasonable hope of benefit. Examples of extraordinary means that I would desire are:

________________________________________

________________________________________

________________________________________

4. If any of the circumstances described in 1, 2, or 3 above exist and I am pregnant, I direct that all medically indicated measures and artificially provided food and water be provided to sustain my life, regardless of my physical or mental condition, if continued medically indicated measures and artificially provided food and water could sustain the life of my unborn child until birth.

D. COPIES

The original or a copy of this document has been given to the following people:

| 1. Name ____________________ | 2. Name ____________________ |
| --- | --- |
| Address ____________________ | Address ____________________ |
| City/State __________________ | City/State __________________ |
| Telephone __________________ | Telephone __________________ |

## Discussion Questions and Projects

1. Explain why our right to life belongs only to God.
2. Show how contraception can lead to abortion and abortion to euthanasia.
3. How is indirect abortion different from direct abortion?
4. Choose two reasons often cited to justify abortion and show how they are false.
5. What consequences would follow making euthanasia legal?
6. What criteria should govern giving narcotics to the dying?
7. List five reasons why euthanasia and physician-assisted suicide are wrong.
8. What are some of the dangers of a living will?
9. What are some of the benefits of a health care proxy?
10. What arguments would you use to persuade your parents or grandparents to draw up an advance medical directive if they have not already done so?

Chapter 9

# Principles Relating to the Preservation of Life

An intervention on the human body affects not only the tissues, the organs, and their functions, but also involves the person himself on different levels. It involves therefore, perhaps in an implicit but nonetheless real way, a moral significance and responsibility. — *Donum Vitae*, Introduction, 3

Having discussed those moral principles relating to the origin of life and the taking of life, we will now consider the moral and ethical guidelines that govern the preservation of life. This category includes such issues as mutilation, sterilization, artificially provided nutrition and hydration, plastic surgery, and tissue and organ transplants.

## Mutilation

**Mutilation is any lessening of the integrity of the human body**. This definition embraces the term in its broadest aspect and is therefore completely comprehensive. Included under it are such widely divergent procedures as tooth extraction, circumcision, and amputation.

A major mutilation is anything which of its very nature renders the individual unfit for natural functions or, in other words, destroys his functional integrity. Examples of major mutilation would include sterilization, removal of the larynx, and removal of the tongue. Theologically, this sort of mutilation would be called "mutilation in the strict sense."

A minor mutilation is any lessening of the sum total of the body which does not destroy its functional integrity. Examples of this would include removal of tonsils or appendix, excision of a uterine tube, or rib resection. The theological term to describe these procedures would be "mutilation in a broad sense."

From a moral perspective, therefore, a distinction must be made between the two types of mutilation, and the distinction is based upon the concept of the functional integrity of the body. By this is meant the degree of completeness necessary for the performance of the functions proper to the body. For example, functional integrity would be destroyed by the amputation of a leg, but the removal of one of two normal kidneys would still leave the degree of completeness necessary for the performance of kidney function.

When mutilation is necessary for the preservation of the life or health of one's own body, it is performed upon the presumed permission of Almighty God, the Supreme Lord of every human being. Detailed discussion of the application of this principle will come in the pages that follow, first regarding the excision or removal of pathologic or diseased organs, which is moral, and then the excision of healthy organs, which is sometimes moral but usually immoral. These principles will be applied to such matters as sterilization, ectopic pregnancies, destruction of fetal life, and plastic surgery.

We will also discuss the donation of a part of one's body to another person to preserve his life or health, such as has been done in the case of kidney transplants.

## Excision of Diseased Organs

Excision of organs that are diseased or pathological is moral and in accord with the natural law since the purpose of such operations is to save the entire body. Since the whole is greater than any of its parts, common sense dictates that the removal of a diseased organ is permissible for the good of the whole body when it cannot be protected by other means. For example, occasionally it becomes necessary to amputate a gangrenous leg so that the life of the patient may be saved. This is an application of the principle of totality discussed earlier in chapter five.

## When Excision of Healthy Organs Is Moral

Surgical removal of a healthy organ from the human body to cure or arrest the further development of disease in another organ may be allowed in certain well-defined cases. Two conditions must exist. First, the preservation or continued functioning of a particular organ must cause serious harm or constitute a threat to the entire body. Second, it must be known that such harm cannot be avoided, or at least notably diminished, except by a mutilation — and the effectiveness of the mutilation must be well established.

The decisive point is not that the organ removed or rendered inoperative is itself diseased, but that its preservation and functioning constitute a serious threat to the whole body. For example, in the case of cancer of the breast, it is permissible to remove one or both ovaries, in spite of the fact that the ovaries are healthy, because the normal functioning of the ovaries could foster the growth of the cancer. Likewise, in the case of cancer of the prostate, removal of one or both testes is permissible.

This conclusion is deduced from the custodial rights over his body which an individual receives from the Creator and is in accordance with the principle of totality, which teaches that every particular organ is subject to the organic whole of the body and must submit to it in case of conflict. This is why surgical removal of a nonpathologic organ to cure or correct disease in another organ is a moral procedure when the requisite conditions are fulfilled.

Another justifying cause for the removal of an apparently healthy organ would be the probability of latent or incipient pathology in the average person. If the mutilation is a minor one, and a reasonable excuse exists for the excision, it would be moral to remove the organ. For example, a normal appendix could be removed during the excision of the gall bladder. This is permitted on the grounds of probability of latent or incipient appendicitis in the average person.

So, too, a man going to a place where proper medical care would be difficult to obtain could have his apparently healthy appendix removed beforehand. For example, a trapper about to leave for a prolonged stay in the Canadian wilderness would be justified in taking such a precaution. But removal of tonsils or a normal appendix is never justified without a sufficient reason for exposing the person to the risks involved in an operation.

Some physicians routinely perform an elective circumcision on male infants. The reason given for this is potential problems with the foreskin. Other doctors do not agree with this custom and maintain that circumcision should not be performed without a medical indication. The arguments in favor of elective circumcision seem rather weak to us.

## Sterilization

Keeping in mind the exceptions we have just explained, we may state the general principle regarding the excision of nonpathologic organs: the removal of a healthy organ is usually immoral. Direct sterilization of the male or female is a case in point.

Sterility is the inability to reproduce. This should not be confused with impotency, which is the impossibility of performing the marriage act. There is a vast and essential moral difference between direct sterilization and indirect sterilization. **Direct sterilization is that which has as its immediate purpose the making of reproduction impossible**. Under this heading fall hysterectomy (removal of the uterus), ligation or cutting of the fallopian tubes in the female, ligation of the vas deferens in the male, removal of the ovaries or the testes, and radiation with x-rays when done solely for the purpose of sterilization.

On the other hand, at times in order to save the health of an individual it may be necessary to perform an operation which results in sterility. This is licit under the principle of the double effect. **Indirect sterilization is that which occurs as a necessary and unintended consequence of a medical procedure which has for its purpose the cure or removal of a pathologic organ**. Indirect sterilization is always moral; direct sterilization is always immoral. This is the essential distinction to keep in mind regarding the morality of sterilization.

We sometimes hear the term "therapeutic sterilization," which is sterilization for the purpose of a cure. This is moral if indirect, that is, if the pathologic condition exists and the operation is performed to save the life or health of the individual concerned. If, however, the so-called therapeutic sterilization is performed to avoid some real or imaginary future illness, it is a direct sterilization and therefore immoral. For example, it is often proposed to sterilize a woman who has no disorder but whose next delivery is expected to be quite difficult. Such a procedure would not be moral because the principle of the twofold effect does not apply.

Ligation of the fallopian tubes to prevent eggs from getting through, or the vas deferens to prevent sperm from getting through, which have as their purpose the avoidance of conception, are immoral. The immorality flows not only from the contraceptive intent, but also from the fact that an unjustified mutilation is performed.

When we consider other means of sterilization, however, it is necessary to make distinctions. Vasectomy, orchidectomy, oophorectomy, salpingectomy, and hysterectomy are sterilizing operations. But such excisions are frequently performed to remove a diseased organ. Here we must apply the principle of the double effect, whereby the excision is allowable because the sterilization only occurs as a concomitant effect of the good action which is performed to eliminate a pathologic condition. In other words, if the operation is performed for the purpose of sterilizing the patient (direct sterilization), it is immoral; but if it is performed to cure or remove a diseased organ (indirect sterilization), it is moral.

It is also moral to remove a healthy organ to save the entire body, as we noted earlier in the case of removing the ovaries to retard breast cancer. This is the principle of totality in action, where one organ is sacrificed for the good of the whole body.

**Punitive sterilization is the sterilizing of a criminal as a punishment, especially for sex crimes**. This is little or no punishment in reality, for the operation in the case of a male is minor and the effect is to make further sex acts "safe" since conception is impossible. Rape, however, is still possible. The morality of such sterilization is under dispute, but we hold that it is immoral.

**Eugenic sterilization is the sterilizing of those who are expected to have defective children**. This is immoral because no authority has such power over the bodies of human beings (cf. *Catechism of the Catholic Church*, n. 2297). Moreover, competent experts on the subject maintain that this type of sterilization would have no appreciable effect in improving the human race.

## Sterilization in Catholic Hospitals

In response to requests from Catholic hospitals about the morality of collaborating in therapeutic sterilization, the Sacred Congregation for the Doctrine of the Faith issued a document (*Haec Sacra Congregatio*) on March 13, 1975 that made the following statement:

> Any sterilization whose sole, immediate effect ... is to render the generative faculty incapable of procreation is to be regarded as direct sterilization, as this is understood in statements of the pontifical Magisterium, especially of Pius XII. It is absolutely forbidden, therefore, according to the teaching of the Church, even when it is motivated by a subjectively right intention of curing or preventing a physical or psychological ill-effect which is foreseen or feared as a result of pregnancy.

The Congregation said that sterilization cannot be justified by the principle of totality because it "does not contribute to the person's integral good," but rather damages that good "since it deprives subsequent freely chosen sexual acts of an essential element." It said that "nothing can justify a Catholic hospital cooperating" in sterilization, and that "cooperation would accord ill with the mission confided to such an institution and would be contrary to the essential proclamation and defense of the moral order."

## Artificial Nutrition/Hydration

In recent years an extensive debate has taken place over the morality of withholding or withdrawing treatment from seriously ill or dying patients. One particular phase of the debate has focused on the withholding or withdrawing of technologically or artificially provided food and water from these patients. For the unconscious, seriously ill and/or dying, the food and water must be provided with the assistance of some form of medical technology, such as an intravenous line, a naso-gastric tube (inserted through the nose), or a gastrostomy (a tube inserted directly into the stomach).

Among the reasons for public confusion about this matter are the high public visibility it has received, the relative lack of understanding of the medical facts, the differing viewpoints of theologians and ethicists, the dilemma for the family in providing long-term care for such a patient, and uncertainty as to whether artificial feeding is an aspect of normal care or whether it is another example of extraordinary medical treatment.

These issues make more difficult the question of moral responsibility on the part of the patient, his or her proxy decision-makers, and the health care professionals as to whether food and water should continue to be provided, albeit by the use of some medical technology.

While the analysis and application of moral principles is relevant to a wide range of cases and medical situations, the primary focus of our discussion will be the permanently unconscious but non-dying patient. In many if not most of the cases given prominence in the courts and the media, this patient has had an accident or otherwise suffered some type of brain damage, rendering him or her unconscious. Emergency medical teams and hospital emergency units generally have used all the available technology to preserve and sustain life so as to assess the patient's actual condition and to restore consciousness.

In the case that we are considering, the diagnostic procedures have determined that the patient will most likely remain permanently unconscious. Such a patient, sometimes described as permanently comatose or as in a persistent vegetative state, suffers from serious brain impairment, is not able to speak, walk, swallow, or perform other customary functions, and has no likelihood of recovery or restoration of function of specific areas of the brain.

However, the brain is not progressively deteriorating and the patient is not dying from some other pathology. In other words, the person is alive but living at a low level of autonomous human functioning. Given basic care, which includes technologically assisted nutrition and hydration, the person could live for many years.

## Some Basic Moral Principles

Within the sphere of Catholic moral thinking, there are some who would permit the discontinuation of food and water in these cases, and there are some who would not. Before discussing the two opposing viewpoints, it is important to state some basic moral principles to which all Catholics should subscribe.

(1) Human life is a precious gift from God, a basic good, and the foundation of other goods.

(2) The human person enjoys a specific relationship with the God who has created and redeemed each of us and calls us to eternal union with him.

(3) We have stewardship over our lives, not absolute dominion, and are thus subject to God's laws regarding human life.

(4) Euthanasia and assisted suicide constitute an unjustifiable destruction of human life and are not morally permissible. Therefore, we may not intend to terminate an innocent person's life by deliberate act or omission, even if he or she is incapacitated.

(5) The quality of a person's life is not the decisive factor in determining the use or non-use of medical or technological means to sustain life.

(6) In deciding on the use of various means of sustaining life, we have customarily referred to a principle based on extraordinary means, that is, we are held to use ordinary means to sustain life, but we are not held to use extraordinary means in every case. This principle was refined in the Holy See's *Declaration on Euthanasia*, which said that medical therapy or technology need not

be used if they are excessively burdensome or provide no benefit to the patient.

(7) Society has a responsibility to protect innocent human life from conception to natural death by its laws and social policies.

## Two Opposing Viewpoints

Within the context of these principles, some would interpret them as saying that our primary responsibility is to pursue the spiritual end of life, which they claim involves some degree of cognitive-affective function. When this function is no longer possible, they argue, it is not necessary to prolong life. In this view, the absence of consciousness would seem to rule out the possibility of pursuing the spiritual end of life and, since the inability to swallow is a pathology from which a person will die, this group would argue that the pathology need not be circumvented by the use of medical technology.

While there is some merit to this argument, there is another group which does not find it convincing. The spiritual end of life, this group says, is certainly union with God, but progress toward that union can be achieved and enhanced even by the unconscious patient if that person had intended that all of his or her suffering or debilitation be offered to God in union with the suffering of Christ.

Furthermore, there have been cases in which the patient was diagnosed as permanently unconscious, but suddenly returned to consciousness, recognized other people, and began to speak rationally and to eat. Accordingly, it is a dangerous precedent to state that apparent absence of cognitive-affective function places a person in a category where there is no obligation on the part of society to sustain his or her life. There are many persons who apparently lack this function, and many more whose cognitive-affective capabilities are so greatly diminished that they can easily be perceived as lacking the ability to pursue the spiritual purposes of life.

A more convincing approach holds that food and water are not primarily forms of therapeutic medical treatment because of and by themselves they will not overcome disease or restore health. Rather, they are basic means of sustaining life without which anyone will die. Thus, nutrition and hydration should be provided as part of a patient's natural care, even if provision of such care requires medical technology, unless or until the benefits of nutrition and hydration are clearly outweighed by a definite danger or burden, or they are clearly useless in sustaining life.

Artificially assisted nutrition and hydration are commonplace but not simple medical procedures. They are not overly expensive; they can generally be monitored by trained persons, including family members; they are not useless in that they sustain the life of the patient; they provide the basic nourishment necessary for life; and they maintain a bond of solidarity between caretakers and the helpless person who is dependent upon them.

The key element in all of this, of course, is intent. If the withholding or withdrawal of nutrition is *intended* to hasten death or to cause death, then it is euthanasia and the withholding or withdrawal of food and water is morally impermissible. In fact, it seems that in many cases those favoring withholding or withdrawal do *intend* to bring the patient's life to an end because of the state of unconsciousness and the lack of any likelihood that consciousness will be regained.

Claiming that the patient is deprived of autonomy and human dignity because of the dependence on medical technology, some argue that there is no point in sustaining life in such circumstances, and they urge withholding or withdrawing technologically provided food and water to bring on death. They further argue that this allows the patient to die with dignity and that it saves family members the cost and emotional burden of long-term care.

What they neglect to point out, however, is that in these cases, discontinuing nutrition and hydration does not simply allow the patient to die from his existing pathology, but introduces a new cause of death — starvation and dehydration!

## Principles to Be Applied in Specific Cases

In light of all that has been said, here are the principles that should be applied to specific cases:

(1) **Unconscious, imminently dying patient** — In the unconscious, imminently dying patient (i.e., progressive and rapid deterioration), the dying process has begun and cannot be reversed. Nutrition and hydration are now useless and, all things considered, no longer a reasonable burden.

(2) **Conscious, imminently dying patient** — In the conscious, imminently dying patient, nutrition and hydration are useless, possibly burdensome, and need not be artificially provided, but may be if desired by the patient.

(3) **Conscious, irreversibly ill, not immediately dying patient** — In the conscious, irreversibly ill, but not imminently dying patient, the person is conscious, beyond cure or reversal of the disease but able to function to some degree. Nutrition and hydration sustain life, so they are not useless, and usually they are not unreasonably burdensome. Nutrition and hydration should be provided unless or until there is clear evidence that provision of food and water is an unreasonable burden for the patient.

(4) **Unconscious, non-dying patient** — "In the unconscious, non-dying patient, nutrition and hydration should be supplied. Feeding is not useless because it sustains a human life. There is no indication that the person is suffering, nor is there any clear evidence that the provision of nutrition and hydration is an unreasonable danger or burden. In such a case, the withdrawal of nutrition/hydration brings about death by starvation and dehydration. Absent any other indication of a definite burden for the patient, withdrawal of nutrition/hydration is not morally justifiable" (Bishop James T. McHugh, *Principles in Regard to Withholding or Withdrawing Artificially Assisted Nutrition / Hydration*, issued by the New Jersey Catholic Conference).

## Plastic Surgery

**Plastic surgery is surgery which aims to repair or restore (chiefly by tissue transfer) parts of the body that have been lost, injured, or deformed**. It is clearly a form of mutilation and as such is governed by the general rules regarding mutilation. There are, however, some specific moral aspects relative to plastic surgery with which we should be familiar.

In general there are three circumstances in which plastic surgery would be employed: to remedy what might truly be called a physical pathologic state (e.g., a skin graft that is necessary after an operation on a tubercular bone in a patient's leg or after a person suffered serious burns in a fire); to change one's physical appearance or enhance beauty; or for psychological reasons. If plastic surgery is clearly indicated for medical reasons, as in the case of the skin grafts mentioned above, there is no moral problem.

In the case of a change of one's physical appearance, purpose and circumstances determine the morality of the surgery. If there are proper safeguards relative to the life and health of the person, if there is a reason sufficiently grave in proportion to the seriousness of the operation, and if the purpose is good, then plastic surgery may be performed in good conscience.

For example, a teacher who is otherwise highly gifted finds that her unpleasant facial characteristics are detrimental to her work. She would be justified in having the defects corrected.

As for psychological considerations, if a feeling of inferiority, a complex, or neurosis could be remedied by plastic surgery, this would not only be morally allowed but also advisable.

Although he made this statement about the moral and spiritual implications of plastic surgery to members of the Italian Association of Plastic Surgeons on October 4, 1958, the words of Pope Pius XII are valid today:

> Christian morality, that looks toward man's ultimate end and embraces and regulates the totality of human values, cannot but assign to physical beauty the place which belongs to it — and that is certainly not at the top of the scale of values since it is neither a spiritual nor an essential good. When the modern development of esthetic surgery seeks the opinion of Christian morals, it does nothing more than ask where in the scale of values physical beauty should be placed.
>
> The morality of actions that are involved in esthetic surgery depends on the concrete circumstances of individual cases. In the moral evaluation of these circumstances, the principal conditions most pertinent to the matter and most determinative in the vast study of cases presented by esthetic surgery are the following: that the intention be good, that the general health of the subject be protected from notable risks, and that the motives be reasonable and proportionate to the "extraordinary means" to which recourse is taken.
>
> Obvious, for example, is the illicitness of an operation sought with the intention of increasing one's own power of seduction and thus inducing others more easily into sin; or exclusively to wrest a guilty person from justice; or an operation damaging to the regular functions of the physical organs; or one desired only through mere vanity or the whims of fashion.
>
> Some disfigurements, or perhaps mere imperfections, are cause of psychic disturbances in a person, or can become an obstacle in social and family relations; or an impediment particularly in people devoted to public life or art in the development of their careers.

> Although the duty to help these patients may belong to many — priests, psychiatrists, friends — when the cause consists of a physical defect which plastic surgery is capable of removing to some degree, no one can deny that a surgical operation is not only medically and esthetically advisable, but is also indicated for spiritual reasons.

In light of these principles enunciated by the Holy Father, second thoughts must be given to the widespread fad of body piercing. Whether it be ear-piercing or piercing other parts of the body, two things should be kept in mind for moral guidance: the underlying medical dangers and any sexual implications.

## Tissue and Organ Transplants

**Tissue transplantation is the transfer of any organized living matter**. Examples of this are blood donations, bone marrow donations, and corneal transplantation. In its broader aspects, tissue transplantation may also include the use of tissue derivatives, such as insulin and testosterone. Transplants may be grouped under three headings: autograft, homograft, and heterograft.

Autograft is the transplantation of one's own tissue, such as a skin graft. It presents no moral problems. Homograft is the transplantation of tissue from one human body to another. Homograft from the dead presents no moral problem, provided that the donor is actually dead and not declared dead prematurely. A corneal transplant from the deceased is an example. Preservation of tissue for future use (bone bank, vascular bank) is also morally permissible.

Any type of tissue transplantation involves mutilation. If the mutilation does not destroy the functional integrity of the donor, it is morally allowable. This would include blood and bone marrow donations and kidney transplants. If, on the other hand, the mutilation destroys the functional integrity of the donor, it is immoral. For example, the donation of both eyes or both kidneys.

Heterograft is the use of tissue or tissue derivatives from a different species (animal to human). The use of tissue derivatives presents no moral problems. Examples include liver extract, insulin, and estrogen. The use of animal tissue, if biologically possible, would also be moral, except in the case of the sex glands or genital organs. This would not be moral because the generative functions of men and women are of an entirely different order from those of animals, involving as they do the procreation not merely of an

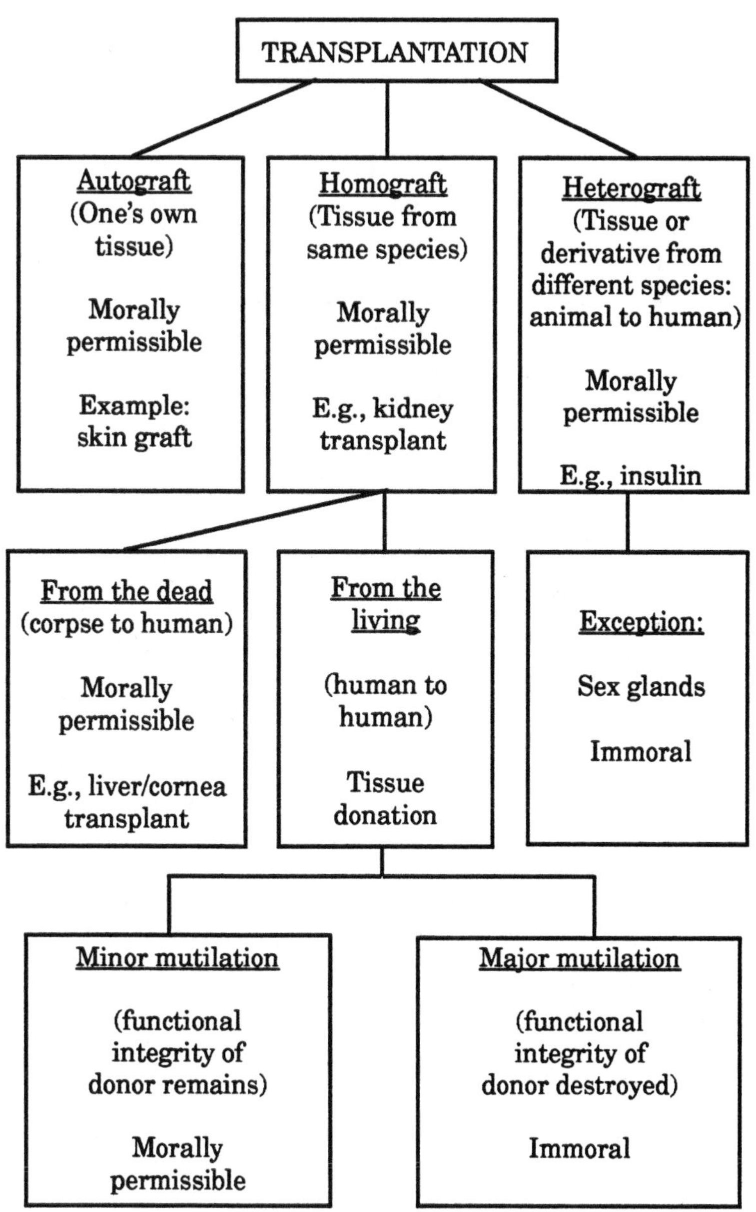


*The Morality of Tissue Transplantation*

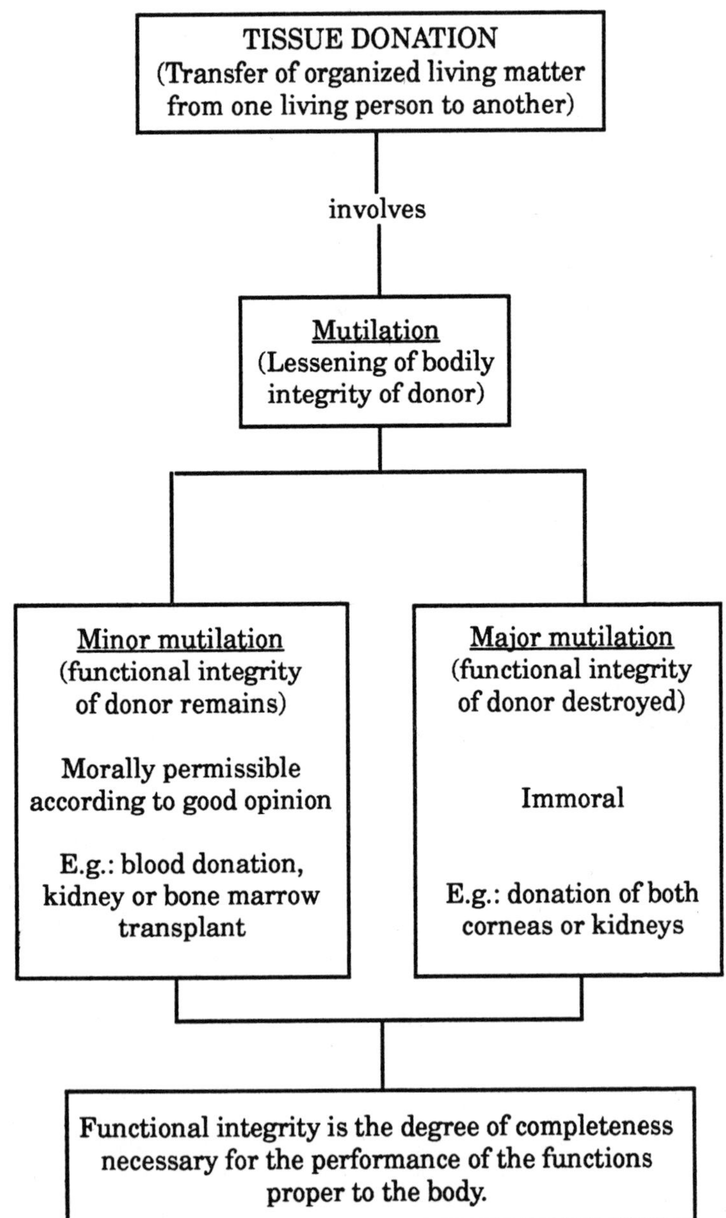


*The Morality of Tissue Donation*

animal body, but also of a human being whose body is united to an immortal soul.

A more recent technological development involves the transplanting of tissue from aborted babies, purportedly for its potential benefit in treating such diseases as Parkinson's and Alzheimer's. Those favoring the use of fetal tissue contend that it is no different ethically from using tissue from murder or accident victims. However, there is a significant difference. The person using the cadavers from murder or accident victims played no part in their deaths, while those using fetal tissue often play a part in the abortion process, either by encouraging a woman to have an abortion (making her think that killing her baby can be a humanitarian act if the baby's tissue can be used to help another person) or by suggesting an abortion procedure that will do the least damage to the unborn child.

One does not need a crystal ball to see how quickly unscrupulous doctors and medical researchers would establish a lucrative market for the harvesting of fetal tissue.

While it is immoral to use tissue obtained from aborted babies, it can be moral to use tissue from miscarriages. There are an estimated 840,700 miscarriages per year in hospitals, according to Dr. Peter Cataldo of the Pope John Center in Brighton, Massachusetts, and about seven to ten percent of them could provide suitable tissue (*Ethics & Medics*, October 1994, p. 4). Efforts are being made to create a network of tissue banks solely using miscarriage tissue.

The Sacred Congregation for the Doctrine of the Faith spelled out the Catholic position on fetal tissue usage in *Donum Vitae*:

> The fruit of human generation, from the first moment of its existence, that is to say, from the moment the zygote has formed, demands the unconditional respect that is morally due to the human being in his bodily and spiritual totality. The human being is to be respected and treated as a person from the moment of conception; and therefore from that same moment his rights as a person must be recognized, among which in the first place is the inviolable right of every innocent human being to life .... The embryo must be treated as a person, it must also be defended in its integrity, tended and cared for, to the extent possible, in the same way as any other human being as far as medical assistance is concerned (Part I, 1).

> The corpses of human embryos and fetuses, whether they have been deliberately aborted or not, must be respected just as the remains of other human beings. In particular, they cannot be subjected to mutilation or to autopsies if their death has not yet been verified and without the consent of the parents or of the mother. Furthermore, the moral requirements must be safeguarded that there be no complicity in deliberate abortion and that the risk of scandal be avoided. Also, in the case of dead fetuses, as for the corpses of adult persons, all commercial trafficking must be considered illicit and should be prohibited (Part I, 4).

## Organ Donation a Good Thing

To donate one's organs after death is a very commendable thing. Of course, informed consent must have been given by the donor or his family, and there must be the certainty that the donor is dead before the organs are removed. Organs can only be harvested from the dead, not from the dying. The long tradition of the Church on this matter, spelled out decades ago by Pope Pius XII and reaffirmed by Pope John Paul II, was reiterated in the *Catechism of the Catholic Church*:

> Organ transplants are not morally acceptable if the donor or those who legitimately speak for him have not given their informed consent. Organ transplants conform with the moral law and can be meritorious if the physical and psychological dangers and risks incurred by the donor are proportionate to the good sought for the recipient. It is morally inadmissible directly to bring about the disabling mutilation or death of a human being, even in order to delay the death of other persons (n. 2296).

In an address sponsored by the Pontifical Academy of Sciences on December 14, 1989, Pope John Paul spoke about the need to establish a precise definition of death "which can be understood and accepted by all." He said that death occurs "when the spiritual principle which ensures the unity of the individual can no longer exercise its functions in and upon the organism, whose elements, left to themselves, disintegrate."

The Holy Father went on to discuss the "tragic dilemma" involved when "it is conceivable that in order to escape certain and imminent death a patient may need to receive an organ which another patient who may be lying next to him in the hospital could provide, but about whose death there still remains some doubt. Consequently, in the process there arises the danger of terminating a human life, of definitively disrupting the psychosomatic unity of a person.

"More precisely, there is a real possibility that the life whose continuation is made unsustainable by the removal of a vital organ may be that of a living person, whereas the respect due to human life absolutely prohibits the direct and positive sacrifice of that life, even though it may be for the benefit of another human being who might be felt to be entitled to preference."

The Pope urged his audience to pursue their "research and studies in order to determine as precisely as possible the exact moment and the indisputable sign of death. For, once such a determination has been arrived at, then the apparent conflict between the duty to respect the life of one person and the duty to effect a cure or even save the life of another disappears. One would be able to know at what moment it would be perfectly permissible to do what had been definitely forbidden previously, namely, the removal of an organ for transplanting, with the best chances of a successful outcome."

Not only is donating organs a good thing, but Pope John Paul equated it with "an everyday heroism made up of gestures of sharing, big and small, which build up an authentic culture of life. A particularly praiseworthy example of such gestures is the donation of organs, performed in an ethically acceptable manner, with a view to offering a chance of health and even of life itself to the sick who sometimes have no other hope" (*Evangelium Vitae*, n. 86).

## Hypnosis

**Hypnosis is an artificially induced state resembling sleep, which is characterized by a particular type of rapport between subject and operator, in which the subject's awareness is narrowed and suggestibility is heightened.** The word "hypnosis" comes from a Greek word meaning "sleep." A hypnotic sleep can be induced by various methods, and the hypnotist is known as the operator. Apparently hypnosis was used from early times, but its formal acceptance as an adjunct to the medical profession is relatively recent.

The exact nature of hypnosis is not known. Various theories which have been proposed to explain it are quite unconvincing. A rather small minority of people apparently cannot be hypnotized. Children between the ages of seven and fourteen — a keen imagination seems to heighten susceptibility — are the most susceptible, while elderly people are the least susceptible. There is no proof that gender is a factor. Psychotics can be hypnotized, although good results are questionable, and lack of voluntary cooperation is not necessarily an impediment to hypnosis.

Dehypnotization offers no serious problems, although an occasional subject will awaken spontaneously at another time. A hypnotist can influence a subject to carry out some action later by making the suggestion while the person is under hypnosis. Obviously this power of the operator carries with it both good and evil potentialities. In practice, the question "What is hypnotism?" is much less important than the question "Who is the hypnotist?"

Hypnosis has been found useful in psychiatry, anesthesia, dentistry, obstetrics, gynecology, and in the treatment of asthma, migraine headaches, nervous tics, and pain relief. Its use as entertainment is wrong. Hypnosis can be used in good conscience when the following conditions are fulfilled:

(1) A serious reason must exist.

(2) The subject's permission should be obtained.

(3) Those conducting the procedure should be of good moral character.

(4) Those conducting the procedure must have proper training and sufficient skill.

Hypnosis in the absence of a witness would not in itself offend morals. However, the presence of a witness is dictated by prudence and is therefore strongly recommended.

## Lie-Detector Tests

Lie-detector (or polygraph) tests are based upon the fact that in most cases the mental reaction of the liar gives rise to concomitant and measurable physical reactions. Under emotional stress, the adrenal glands produce epinephrine (adrenalin) in increased amounts. This causes immediate but transitory reactions: the blood vessels contract, raising the blood pressure sharply; the heart rate increases; muscles contract, causing the skin to become taut; respirations become rapid and labored.

Since these symptoms disappear quickly, their relationship to a series of questions can be recorded graphically. This is accomplished by means of electronic detectors which record the various impulses on a moving tape. The result is a graph which can be read and studied by an expert examiner. In general, the process resembles an electrocardiogram.

When lie-detector tests are given, the operator marks a graph to correlate each question with the concomitant physical reactions. A series of test questions establishes the general pattern of the subject's reactions. Questions are so framed that the answers are simply yes or no. There is no moral problem connected with the taking of such measurements and, when the subject consents, a polygraph test may be used without sin.

We might ask, however, whether it is morally right to oblige an individual to undergo a lie-detector test. Generally speaking, the answer is no. A person is not obliged by moral law (or by civil law) to be a witness against himself, or to turn himself over to civil authority for punishment. Undergoing a polygraph test would be equivalent to doing just that. Therefore, one is ordinarily not morally bound to submit to such a test, nor would it be right for those in authority to force such a test upon an individual.

Under the natural law, if our refusal would bring grave harm to a third party or to the common good, we might be obliged to take the test. However, we are permitted by moral law to take advantage of the legal safeguards offered us by civil law. A lie-detector test would be used only in connection with civil procedure or with the sanction of civil law. If no such requirement is imposed by civil law, then the individual has no moral obligation to submit to such a test.

## Alcoholism

The abuse of alcohol involves physical, mental, and spiritual considerations. It is a mistake to ignore any of these three aspects of the problem because an effective solution to alcoholism depends on the adjustment of one's personality on all three levels. We must not fall victim to the modern error that all drinkers are merely sick and are therefore not responsible for their condition and not capable of stopping their evil practices. If all who abuse alcohol are nothing but the innocent victims of an unpleasant disease, how can the Bible threaten them with severe punishment? No drunkards, said St. Paul, "will inherit God's kingdom" (1 Corinthians 6:10).

There is a difference between true alcoholics and so many who abuse alcohol. Certainly we should be charitable to all, but to hold all blameless is not charity. Such an attitude merely furnishes them with an excuse and lessens their chances of reform or of a cure. Every victim of drink, whether physically ill or just morally deficient, must contribute to his own recovery by the exercise of his God-given faculty of free will unless, in a rare case, he is so physically impelled toward liquor that he no longer retains the use of reason and free will.

The famous organization known as Alcoholics Anonymous has enjoyed notable success in working with those addicted to alcohol. Their "Twelve Steps," which are patterned on the Ten Commandments and which were authored in part by Fr. Edward Dowling, a Jesuit priest, are worthy of consideration:

(1) We admitted we were powerless over alcohol — that our lives had become unmanageable.

(2) Came to believe that a Power greater than ourselves could restore us to sanity.

(3) Made a decision to turn our will and our lives over to the care of God as we understood Him.

(4) Made a searching and fearless moral inventory of ourselves.

(5) Admitted to God, to ourselves, and to another human being the exact nature of our wrongs.

(6) Were entirely ready to have God remove all these defects of character.

(7) Humbly asked Him to remove our shortcomings.

(8) Made a list of all persons we had harmed and became willing to make amends to them all.

(9) Made direct amends to such people wherever possible, except when to do so would injure them or others.

(10) Continued to take personal inventory and when we were wrong promptly admitted it.

(11) Sought through prayer and meditation to improve our conscious contact with God as we understood Him, praying only for knowledge of His will for us and the power to carry that out.

(12) Having had a spiritual awakening as the result of these steps, we tried to carry this message to alcoholics and to practice these principles in all our affairs.

## Drug Addiction

Drug addiction, like alcoholism, also involves physical, mental and spiritual considerations. But while the physical and mental aspects are ordinarily recognized, the spiritual is frequently ignored. In light of the crisis that drug addiction brings to a human life, the need for spiritual assistance should never be minimized.

It is not within the scope of this book to treat the complicated aspects of alcoholism and drug addiction, but if the problem arises, seek help from a priest or a counsellor, who can then refer the person to an appropriate specialist so that all the necessary assistance can be provided. AA's 12-step program can be applied to drug addicts, too.

## AIDS

Acquired Immune Deficiency Syndrome (AIDS) has become more and more of a threat to society as people jeopardize their own physical well-being, and that of others, through immoral behavior. Certainly the grace of God can give extra strength and a spirit of Christian resignation to AIDS victims and their families, and every Christian has an obligation to show compassion and love for those afflicted with this disease.

However, while loving the sinner and working and praying for his spiritual conversion, we cannot remain silent in the face of a widespread and false propaganda campaign relative to the transmission of AIDS. There are some who have contracted the disease innocently through such means as bad blood transfusions, but the major cause of the spread of AIDS is immoral sexual behavior and the illicit use of drugs.

Those waging the propaganda campaign insist that promiscuous sexual conduct can continue if only "proper precautions" are taken, meaning the use of condoms during sodomy. This is a foolish and irresponsible solution, not only because it takes no account of the immoral nature of the behavior, but also because condoms, which have a significant failure rate when used in heterosexual intercourse, have an even higher failure rate when used in homosexual intercourse.

The Catholic Church does not and cannot condone the use of condoms as a means of stemming the spread of AIDS. Nor does the Church approve the practice of making sterile needles available to drug addicts. Not only are these approaches immoral, but they send the wrong message to the population at large, and especially to the young, namely, that promiscuity and drug abuse are acceptable as long as the proper precautions are taken.

It should be obvious in society today that sexual activity outside the framework of marriage is destructive of the individual and of the community as well. Only abstinence from the improper

## Discussion Questions and Projects

1. Show the distinction between mutilation that is morally permissible and that which is not permissible.

2. Why does the Church oppose the sterilization of males and females?

3. Should rapists be sterilized?

4. Should those who might have defective children be sterilized?

5. When is withdrawal of artificial nutrition/hydration permissible?

6. Under what conditions may a person undergo plastic surgery?

7. What is wrong with transplanting tissue obtained from aborted babies?

8. Under what conditions may a person be hypnotized?

9. Which of AA's twelve steps is the most important and why?

10. Why can't so-called "safe sex" bring about an end to AIDS and other sexually transmitted diseases?

11. Take one of the basic moral issues discussed in the chapter and write a 300-word paper explaining and defending the Church's position.

# PART III

# SPIRITUAL HELP FOR AND WITH THE SICK

Illness can lead to anguish, self-absorption, sometimes even despair and revolt against God. It can also make a person more mature, helping him discern in his life what is not essential so that he can turn toward that which is. Very often illness provokes a search for God and a return to him.

— *Catechism of the Catholic Church*, n. 1501

Chapter 10

# Never Forget the Spiritual

"When I am completely united to you, there will be no more sorrow or trials; entirely full of you, my life will be complete." — St. Augustine as quoted in the *Catechism of the Catholic Church*, n. 45

A certain few problems, old but ever new, have constantly been the source of discussion among people of every age, tantalizing Greek philosophers of old and the serious thinkers of modern times. One of these problems is the mystery of suffering. Why was this child born deaf and blind? Why is it that often the good suffer and the bad prosper? Why does that aged patient who has outlived all her loved ones linger on alone in her misery? Why are so many people mentally afflicted? Why does God permit evil and suffering?

At some time in our lives we might be called upon to help a person resign himself to suffering, to prolonged confinement, or even to death. Occasionally one finds it necessary to console or admonish a family in the face of a great trial. In such situations, the most valuable help comes from the one who by reading, experience, and prayer has learned Christianity's answer to the problem of suffering and has allowed that answer to penetrate deep into his or her soul.

One should lose no opportunity to read on this subject and to ponder over it (cf. Pope John Paul's apostolic letter *On the Christian Meaning of Human Suffering* and Peter Kreeft's book *Making Sense Out of Suffering*). Especially should be treasured the wisdom of those who are close to God because a fuller comprehension of the problem of suffering is the reward of holiness and the fruit of long experience.

## Christ's Answer to Suffering

The hedonists who lived before Christ recoiled from suffering, vainly offering the standard that pleasure should be the chief good in life. But that selfish philosophy was little help for most of humanity, which despite its efforts could not escape all suffering. That is why the Greek writers Sophocles and Euripides called life a misfortune. It is said that a pagan philosopher at his wit's end exclaimed: "The best thing in the world is not to be born; the next best, if we have to be born, is to die as quickly as possible." But this pagan answer was most inadequate.

Even the Jews, God's chosen people, although they saw suffering in a different light from the pagans, did not have a satisfactory explanation for the mystery of suffering. Some of them believed that any suffering, any affliction, was a punishment for sin. It was necessary for Jesus to change this belief.

Recall the time that a group gathered around a blind man asked Jesus, "Rabbi, was it his sin or that of his parents that caused him to be born blind?" And Jesus answered: "Neither. It was no sin, either of this man or of his parents. Rather, it was to let God's works show forth in him" (John 9:2-3). Our Lord then gave the man back his sight.

The key to the suffering and afflictions of this life can be found in Christ's answer to his questioners. Such trials are sent or allowed by God, but not necessarily as a punishment. Sometimes they are a blessing in disguise. The Christian explanation of suffering was summed up by St. Peter:

> If you do wrong and get beaten for it, what credit can you claim? But if you put up with suffering for doing what is right, this is acceptable in God's eyes. It was for this you were called, since Christ suffered for you in just this way and left you an example, to have you follow in his footsteps (1 Peter 2:20-21).

If, then, we are to call ourselves Christians — followers of Christ — we may expect to find some trials in our life.

## The Example of the Cross

In times past the image of the cross was inseparable from the life of a Christian. The Apostles, gloriously spurred on by the figure of the crucified Christ, did not hesitate to hold up this symbol of our salvation: "We preach Christ crucified."

Today, however, the cross finds no intimate place in the lives of many people, even some who call themselves Christians. It is spurned in public life, banned from schools and offices, and even torn down from hilltops lest it offend those who do not believe in Christ. One exception was a young woman doctor who, after completing her internship and starting her own practice, placed a large crucifix on the wall of her office. Some patients were surprised at first, but as she spoke with them it became an inspiration to them and a source of encouragement as they recognized the connection between the cross and the doctor's medical and scientific knowledge.

## Giving in Order to Get

Have you ever stopped to consider how many times in life we have to give something — time, study, training, hard work — before we can attain a desired goal? That is, of course, true when we purchase some article at the mall, but it is also true in a deeper and wider sense. The fact that we usually give in order to get is true in the spiritual order as well as in the material order.

In the case of knowledge, for instance, a person who has mastered astronomy or mathematics or medicine has given much energy and has sacrificed a great deal to gain the knowledge necessary to excel in one of these fields. A teacher will tell you that she never profited so much from her subject when she merely studied it as when she began to teach it. It is when one begins to teach a subject, and religion is no exception, that one really gains a deep knowledge and appreciation of it.

We all know the joy of giving something that makes another person happy. Love is like that. A person's love grows and deepens as he gives and sacrifices for the one he loves. The cliche that one gets more from giving than from receiving is true.

The same principle applies to our relationship with God. That is why suffering, sacrifice, penance, and generosity to God are necessary to obtain real happiness and a shower of graces. That is why, if we live our life as Christ intended we should, there will be suffering involved, but as St. Paul said, if we suffer with Christ, we will be "glorified with him. I consider the sufferings of the present to be as nothing compared with the glory to be revealed in us" (Romans 8:17-18).

In the ordinary fulfilling of the duties of our state in life, there will be crosses, and the submissive, willing, and joyful acceptance of those crosses will bring us great blessings from God. When we say the Lord's Prayer, we say, "Thy will be done," but do we mean it? If we do, then we will carry out God's will for us every day, and offer up whatever difficulties that may pose. The spirit of resignation to those trials God sends us can develop into courageous, even joyous endurance.

We try to see the value of these trials in Christ's plan. We see the fruits of patience, love, and perseverance; we see a means of atoning for sin and shortening purgatory, either for ourselves or for others; we see a means of becoming more Christ-like; we see the fruit of love tested by trials blossoming in our soul as it did for the repentant sinful woman at our Lord's feet: "I tell you, that is why her many sins are forgiven — because of her great love. Little is forgiven the one whose love is small" (Luke 7:47).

When crosses come then, our reaction should not be "Why did God do this to me?" but rather "Thy will be done." For in God's plan suffering should not be seen as a punishment but as a gift from God to those he loves in a special way. If we suffer with him, as St. Paul said, we will also reign with him. For every sorrowful mystery there is a joyful mystery. For every Good Friday there is an Easter Sunday.

There is often a darker and a lighter side in the events of our lives. At the Annunciation, the Blessed Virgin Mary was "deeply troubled" at the angel's words (Luke 1:29), but later experienced peace and happiness. She suffered the anguish of losing Jesus in the temple when he was twelve years old, but experienced the joy of finding him again. She stood in agony at the foot of the cross on Good Friday, but exulted at the resurrection on the third day.

## More Insights into Evil and Suffering

The presence of evil and suffering in the world will not be truly understood by us until the final judgment at the end of time. But Holy Scripture and the teaching of the Church can shed some light on this mystery. Consider the following points:

(1) God created the first humans in a state of holiness, but Adam and Eve, at the urging of Satan, set themselves against God and brought evil into the world. As a result of their sin, said Vatican II, people "have frequently fallen into multiple errors .... The result has been the corruption of morals and human institutions and not rarely contempt for the human person himself" (*Decree on the Apostolate of the Laity*, n. 7). Thus, the evils of the world are traceable not to God but to original sin and our personal sins.

(2) While God is not the cause of evil and suffering, he permits these afflictions in order to draw some good out of them. For instance, out of the suffering and death of Jesus came eternal salvation. If Jesus did not die on the cross, we could not get to heaven.

(3) If we join our sufferings with those of Christ, they will bring us closer to him. Who knows more about homelessness and poverty than our Lord, who was born in a stranger's cave and buried in a stranger's grave? Who knows more about loneliness than our Lord, who was abandoned by all his friends? Who knows more about injustice than our Lord, who was falsely accused and wrongly convicted of criminal activity? Who knows more about physical and mental pain than our Lord, who underwent excruciating torture and death?

(4) In his apostolic letter "On the Christian Meaning of Human Suffering" (*Salvifici Doloris*), Pope John Paul said that "suffering is present in the world in order to release love, in order to give birth to works of love toward neighbor, in order to transform the whole of human civilization into a 'civilization of love' " (n. 30). Thus, suffering can be beneficial if it stirs in us a spirit of compassion, love, and sacrifice toward others.

## Suffering and Happiness

In our relations with God there has always been, strangely enough, some connection between suffering and happiness. From a heart that had known the heavy weight of sorrow, the poet Joyce Kilmer expressed this beautiful paradox:

> Lo, comfort blooms on pain, and peace on strife,
> And gain on loss!
> What is the key to everlasting life?
> A blood-stained cross.

For those who are suffering, for those whose task it is to care for the suffering, for relatives who are torn by watching a loved one suffer, the conviction of faith that suffering can strengthen, can purify, can bring one closer to Christ in his suffering can give a new dimension to this inescapable fact of life. The compassionate words of Pope John Paul, in a talk to the sick on May 28, 1982, are worthy of our meditation:

> There is no force or power that can block God's love for you. Sickness and suffering seem to contradict all that is worthy,

all that is desired by man. And yet no disease, no injury, no infirmity can ever deprive you of your dignity as children of God and brothers and sisters of Jesus Christ.

By his dying on the cross, Christ shows us how to make sense of our suffering. In his Passion, we find the inspiration and strength to turn away from any temptation to resentment, and grow through pain into a new life.

Suffering is an invitation to be more like the Son in doing the Father's will. It offers us an opportunity to imitate Christ who died to redeem mankind from sin. Thus, the Father has disposed that suffering can enrich the individual and the whole Church.

## Discussion Questions and Projects:

1. Why does God permit people to suffer?
2. Can we expect to escape all suffering in this life?
3. Why did Jesus suffer such a terrible death on the cross? Couldn't he have accomplished our redemption in an easier way?
4. What did Jesus mean when he said that if we want to come after him, we must pick up our cross and follow in his steps?
5. What are some of the crosses people have to carry in this life?
6. Give three examples of good things that can come out of suffering.
7. What did St. Paul mean when he said, "I consider the sufferings of the present to be as nothing compared with the glory to be revealed in us"?
8. Write a 200-word paper on the sufferings experienced by St. Paul during his missionary journeys.

Epilogue

# Pope John Paul II

In a society like today's, then, which claims to thrive on well-being and on consumerism, and where everything is valued on the basis of efficiency and profit, the problem of sickness and of suffering, which cannot be denied, is either "removed" or people think that it can be resolved by relying exclusively on the means offered by advanced modern technology.

All of this constitutes a veritable "challenge" for those who profess to be believers and who have from revelation, and above all from the Gospel, an answer to welcome into their own lives and to offer to the world as a sign of hope and as a light which gives meaning to existence. This is the "wood of the cross."

Christian faith — and it is not alone here — affirms the continuation of man's spiritual principle beyond death. However, this state of "beyond" for those who do not have faith is without a clear face or form, and everyone feels anguish when confronted by a separation which so brutally contradicts our will to live, our wish to exist. Unlike animals, man knows that he must die and he perceives this as an affront to his dignity. Although in the flesh he is mortal, he also realizes that he ought not to die because he carries within himself an openness, an aspiration towards the eternal.

Why does death exist? What is its meaning? Christian faith affirms that there is a mysterious link between death and moral disorder or sin. Yet at the same time, faith imbues death with a positive meaning because it has the resurrection as its horizon. It shows us the Word of God who takes on our mortal condition and offers his life in sacrifice for sinners on the cross.

Death is neither a simple physical consequence nor a mere punishment. It becomes the gift of self for the sake of love. In the risen Christ we see death definitively conquered: "Death has no more dominion over him" (Rom. 6:9). The Christian also confidently looks forward to regaining his own personal totality, transfigured and definitively possessed in Christ (cf. 1 Cor. 15:22).

Such is death seen through the eyes of faith. It is not so much an end of living as an entry into a new life, a life without end. If we freely accept the love which God offers us, we will have a new birth in joy and in light, a new *dies natalis* [birthday].

—*L'Osservatore Romano*, January 8, 1990

# PRAYERS FOR THE

# SICK AND DYING

### Prayer in Honor of Saint Luke for Doctors

Good Saint Luke, who combined a physician's knowledge with faith in Jesus and love for his mother, obtain for doctors great medical skill, lively divine faith, and a spirit of kindness and charity, through Christ our Lord. Amen.

### Prayer in Honor of Saint Camillus

O God, who gave Saint Camillus the grace to nurse the sick with true Christian charity, grant through his intercession that I may help the sick in a manner pleasing to you, and so merit an eternal reward, through Christ our Lord. Amen.

### Prayer for a Newborn Baby

O holy infant Jesus, lover of children, bless this little infant newly born into the world. Strengthen his (her) body by your power, and in your loving kindness refresh his (her) soul by the saving waters of Baptism that he (she) may be destined for an eternal union with you. Amen.

### Prayer for a Sick Child

Father of mercies and God of all consolation, who pours forth your healing grace on bodies as well as souls, deign to raise up this sick child and restore him (her) to your holy Church and to his (her) parents, so that his (her) life being prolonged, advancing in grace and wisdom before you and before the world, he (she) may serve you in justice and holiness and express due gratitude for your mercy, through Christ our Lord. Amen.

### Prayer for a Sick Person

O holy Lord, Father almighty, eternal God, pour out your gracious blessing upon the sick. Graciously draw near at the invocation of your name so that, having freed your servant from sickness and having given him (her) health, you may raise him (her) up by your right hand, strengthen him (her) by your power, and restore him (her) to your holy Church. Amen.

**Prayer for All the Sick**

O God of the heavenly virtues, who drives all sickness and all infirmity from the bodies of men and women by the power of your word, graciously draw near to your sick servants, that with weakness put to flight and health and strength continually renewed, they may ever bless your holy name. Amen.

**Prayer to Be Said by a Sick Person**

My God, I believe in you, I hope in you, I love you above all things with all my soul, with all my heart, and with all my strength. I love you because you are infinitely good and worthy of being loved and, because I love you, I repent with all my heart of having offended you. Have mercy on me, a sinner. Amen.

**Prayer for a Patient Who Has Received Communion**

O holy Lord, Father almighty, eternal God, we earnestly beseech you that the most sacred Body of our Lord Jesus Christ, your Son, which our brother (sister) has received, may be an eternal remedy for him (her) both in body and in soul. Amen.

**Prayer for a Person Who Has Received the Sacrament of the Sick**

Lord God, you have spoken through your Apostle James, saying: "Is anyone sick? He should call in the priests of the Church and have them pray over him and anoint him with oil in the name of the Lord. That prayer, said with faith, will save the sick person, and the Lord will restore him to health. If he has committed sins, they will be forgiven him." We beseech you, our Redeemer, to cure by the grace of the Holy Spirit the ailments of this sick man (woman). Heal his (her) wounds and forgive his (her) sins. Alleviate all his (her) physical and mental sufferings and mercifully restore him (her) to good health, so that, having recovered through your mercy, he (she) may return to his (her) former duties. Amen.

## Prayer for a Person in Imminent Danger of Death

O most gracious God, Father of mercies and God of all consolation, who wills that no one should perish who believes and trusts in you, in your great mercy look kindly upon your servant whom true faith and Christian hope commend to you. Visit him (her) with your saving power and, through the Passion and death of your only begotten Son, graciously grant to him (her) pardon and remission of all his (her) sins. May his (her) soul at the hour of its departure find you a merciful judge. Cleansed from every stain by the blood of your Son, may he (she) be worthy to pass into life everlasting, through Christ our Lord. Amen.

## Prayer for All the Dying

O most merciful Jesus, lover of souls, I pray you by the agony of your most Sacred Heart, and by the sorrows of your Immaculate Mother, cleanse in your own blood the sinners of the whole world who are now in agony and who are to die this day. Amen. Heart of Jesus, once in agony, have pity on the dying. Amen.

## Litany of the Dying

Lord, have mercy.
Christ, have mercy.
Lord, have mercy.
Holy Mary, pray for him (her).
All you holy angels and archangels, pray for him (her).
Holy Abel, pray for him (her).
All you choirs of the just, pray for him (her).
Holy Abraham, pray for him (her).
St. John the Baptist, pray for him (her).
St. Joseph, pray for him (her).
All you holy patriarchs and prophets, pray for him (her).
St. Peter, pray for him (her).
St. Paul, pray for him (her).
St. Andrew, pray for him (her).
St. John, pray for him (her).
All you holy Apostles and evangelists, pray for him (her).
All you holy disciples of our Lord, pray for him (her).
All you holy innocents, pray for him (her).

St. Stephen, pray for him (her).
St. Lawrence, pray for him (her).
All you holy martyrs, pray for him (her).
St. Sylvester, pray for him (her).
St. Gregory, pray for him (her).
St. Augustine, pray for him (her).
All you holy bishops and confessors, pray for him (her).
St. Benedict, pray for him (her).
St. Francis, pray for him (her).
St. Camillus, pray for him (her).
St. John of God, pray for him (her).
All you holy monks and hermits, pray for him (her).
St. Mary Magdalen, pray for him (her).
St. Lucy, pray for him (her).
All you holy virgins and widows, pray for him (her).
All you holy saints of God, intercede for him (her).

Be merciful, spare him (her), O Lord.
Be merciful, deliver him (her), O Lord.
From your anger, deliver him (her), O Lord.
From death's dangers, deliver him (her), O Lord.
From an unholy death, deliver him (her), O Lord.
From the punishments of hell, deliver him (her), O Lord.
From every evil, deliver him (her), O Lord.
From the power of the devil, deliver him (her), O Lord.

Through your birth, deliver him (her), O Lord.
Through your cross and Passion, deliver him (her), O Lord.
Through your death and burial, deliver him (her), O Lord.
Through your glorious Resurrection, deliver him (her), O Lord.
Through your wonderful Ascension, deliver him (her), O Lord.
Through the grace of the Holy Spirit, the Consoler, deliver him (her), O Lord.
In the day of judgment, deliver him (her), O Lord.

We who are sinners, we implore you, hear us.
That you would spare him (her), we implore you, hear us.

Lord, have mercy.
Christ, have mercy.
Lord, have mercy.

**Let us pray.**

To you do I turn for refuge, St. Joseph, patron of the dying, at whose happy deathbed Jesus and Mary stood watch. Because of this twofold pledge of hope, I earnestly commend to you the soul of this servant in his (her) last agony, so that he (she) may, with you as protector, be set free from the snares of the devil and from everlasting death, and may attain to everlasting joy, through Christ our Lord. Amen.

## My Daily Prayer (To Be Said by Dying Persons)

I believe in one God. I believe that God rewards the good and punishes the wicked. I believe that in God there are three divine Persons — God the Father, God the Son, and God the Holy Spirit.

I believe that God the Son became man, without ceasing to be God. I believe that he is my Lord and my Savior, the Redeemer of the human race, that he died on the cross for the salvation of all, that he died also for me. I believe on God's authority everything he has taught and revealed.

O my God, give me strong faith. O my God, help me to believe with lively faith. O my God, who are all good and merciful, I sincerely hope to be saved. Help me to do all that is necessary for my salvation.

I have committed many sins in my life, but now I turn away from them and hate them. I am sorry, truly sorry, for all of them because I have offended you, my God, who are all good and all perfect, all-holy, all-merciful and kind, and who died on the cross for me.

I love you, O my God, with all my heart. Please forgive me for having offended you. I promise, O God, that with your help, I will never offend you again. My God, have mercy on me. Amen.

# Bibliography

(The following materials include Catholic, non-Catholic, and medical references and sources for further reading. The authors do not necessarily agree with everything which might be treated in them.)

*Abortion and the Constitution*. Edited by Dennis J . Horan, Edward R. Grant, and Paige C. Cunningham
Alcorn, Randy. *Pro-Life Answers to Pro-Choice Arguments*
Arras, T., and Steinbock, B. *Ethical Issues in Modern Medicine*

Brennan, William. *The Abortion Holocaust*

*Catechism of the Catholic Church*
*Catholic Encyclopedia*. Edited by Fr. Peter M.J. Stravinskas
Clowes, Brian. *The Facts of Life*
*Code of Canon Law*
Connell, Francis J. *Outlines of Moral Theology*
*Contemporary Issues in Bioethics*. Edited by T. Beauchamp and L. Walters

DeMarco, Donald. *Biotechnology and the Assault on Parenthood*
Dilenno, Joseph A., M.D., and Smith, Herbert F., S.J. *Homosexuality: The Questions*
*Documents of Vatican II, The*. Edited by Walter M. Abbott, S.J.
Drummey, James J. *Catholic Replies*

Everett, Carol. *Blood Money: Getting Rich off a Woman's Right to Choose*

Flynn, E. *Issues in Medical Ethics*
Ford, J. *The Hospital Prayer Book*

Goodfrield, J. *Playing God*
Grant, George. *Grand Illusion: The Legacy of Planned Parenthood*
Gratsch, E. *Aquinas' Summa: An Introduction and Interpretation*

Grisez, Germain. *Christian Moral Principles*
_________. *Difficult Moral Questions*
_________. *Living a Christian Life*

Hardon, John A., S.J. *The Catholic Catechism*
_________. *Modern Catholic Dictionary*
_________. *The Question and Answer Catholic Catechism*
Harvey, John F., O.S.F.S. *The Homosexual Person: New Thinking in Pastoral Care*
_________. *The Truth About Homosexuality*
Hayes, Fr. Edward J., Hayes, Msgr. Paul J. and Drummey, James J. *Catholicism and Life*
_________. *Catholicism and Reason*
_________. *Catholicism and Society*

John Paul II, Pope. "On the Christian Meaning of Suffering" (*Salvifici Doloris*)
_________. *Crossing the Threshold of Hope*
_________. "The Gospel of Life" (*Evangelium Vitae*)
_________. "The Role of the Christian Family in the Modern World" (*Familiaris Consortio*)
_________. "The Splendor of Truth" (*Veritatis Splendor*)
John XXIII, Pope. "Christianity and Social Progress" (*Mater et Magistra*)
Jurgens, William A. *The Faith of the Early Fathers* (3 vols.)

Kasun, Jacqueline. *The War Against Population*
Kearon, Kenneth. *Medical Ethics: An Introduction*
Kippley, John F. *Sex and the Marriage Covenant*
___________. and Kippley, Sheila. *The Art of Natural Family Planning*
Kreeft, Peter. *Making Choices*
_________. *Making Sense Out of Suffering*

Lawler, Ronald, Boyle, Joseph and May, William E. *Catholic Sexual Ethics*

Marshall, R.G., and Donovan, C.A. *Blessed Are the Barren: The Social Policy of Planned Parenthood*
May, G., M.D. *Addiction and Grace*
May, William E. *Human Existence, Medicine and Ethics*
_________. *An Introduction to Moral Theology*

McFadden, C. *Medical Ethics*
McHugh, Bishop James T. *Principles in Regard to Withholding Artificially Assisted Nutrition / Hydration*
Minogue, B. *Bioethics: A Committee Approach*
Munson, R. *Intervention and Reflection: Basic Issues in Medical Ethics*
Myers, Bishop John M. *The Obligations of Catholics and the Rights of Unborn Children*

Nathanson, Bernard N., M.D. *Aborting America*
_________. *The Hand of God*
National Conference of Catholic Bishops. *Ethical and Religious Directives for Catholic Health Care Services*

O'Connor, Cardinal John J. *Abortion: Questions and Answers*
O'Donnell, T. *Medicine and Christian Morality*

Paul VI, Pope. "On Human Life" (*Humanae Vitae*)
Pius XI, Pope. "On Christian Marriage" (*Casti Connubii*)
Pius XII, Pope. *The Human Body* (Over 90 allocutions on medical ethics)
Pontifical Council for the Family. *The Truth and Meaning of Human Sexuality*
Pontifical Council for Pastoral Assistance. *Charter for Health Care Workers*

Reardon, David C. *Aborted Women: Silent No More*
Rescher, N. *Unpopular Essays on Technological Progress*
Rice, Charles E. *50 Questions on Abortion, Euthanasia and Related Issues*
_________. *50 Questions on the Natural Law*
_________. *No Exception: A Pro-Life Imperative*
Rini, Suzanne. *Beyond Abortion: A Chronicle of Fetal Experimentation*

Sacred Congregation for the Doctrine of the Faith. *Declaration on Certain Problems of Sexual Ethics*
_________. *Declaration on Euthanasia*
_________. *Declaration on Procured Abortion*
_________. *Instruction on Respect for Human Life in Its Origins and on the Dignity of Procreation*
_________. *Letter to Bishops of the Catholic Church on the Pastoral Care of Homosexual Persons*

Schonborn, C. *From Death to Life: The Christian Journey*
Sheed, Frank. *Theology and Sanity*
Smith, Herbert F., S.J. *Pro-Choice? Pro-Life?*
Smith, Janet E. *Humanae Vitae: A Generation Later*
Smith, Wesley J. *Forced Exit: The Slippery Slope from Assisted Suicide to Legalized Murder*

Thayer, Linda. *AIDS & Adolescents*

*Vatican Council II: The Conciliar and Post Conciliar Documents*. Edited by Austin Flannery, O.P.
Veatch, R. *Medical Ethics*

Wertham, Frederic, M.D. *The German Euthanasia Program*
_________. *A Sign for Cain*
*Why Humanae Vitae Was Right, A Reader*. Edited by Janet E. Smith
Willke, Dr. and Mrs. J.C. *Abortion: Questions and Answers*
Wuerl, Donald W., Lawler, Thomas C. and Lawler, Ronald, O.F.M., Cap. *The Catholic Catechism*
_________. *The Teaching of Christ*

# *Index*